# ESSENTIAL ITALIAN GRAMMAR

This book is designed specifically for those with limited learning time who want to be able to speak and understand simple, everyday Italian. It is not a condensed outline of Italian grammar, teaching how to construct sentences from rules and vocabulary, but a series of aids and selected points of grammar enabling the student to use Italian phrases and words more effectively and with greater versatility. Thus, although no previous knowledge of Italian grammar is assumed, the student should be familiar with a number of phrases and expressions such as may be found in any phrase book.

The grammatical rules and forms fundamental to the structure of the Italian language are presented in logical sequence and with such clarity that most of them can be memorised in a single reading. Each point is illustrated with useful phrases and sentences, and there is a separate section on grammatical terms.

The ideal supplement to a phrase book for the beginner, *Essential Italian Grammar* will also be valuable as a refresher course and to those attending Italian conversation classes.

D1342134

TEACH YOURSELF BOOKS

*Also in this series*

ESSENTIAL GERMAN GRAMMAR
ESSENTIAL SPANISH GRAMMAR
ESSENTIAL FRENCH GRAMMAR

# ESSENTIAL ITALIAN GRAMMAR

Olga Ragusa

TEACH YOURSELF BOOKS
Hodder and Stoughton

*First published by Dover Publications Inc. in 1963*
*Teach Yourself Books edition 1975*
*Ninth Impression 1986*
*Reissued in this format 1988*

ISBN 0 340 49696 7

*Printed and bound in Great Britain for*
*Hodder and Stoughton Educational,*
*a division of Hodder and Stoughton Ltd,*
*Mill Road, Dunton Green, Sevenoaks, Kent,*
*by Richard Clay Ltd, Bungay, Suffolk*

# Contents

# Introduction

*Essential Italian Grammar* is based on the assumption that you plan to spend a limited number of hours studying Italian grammar and that your objective is simple everyday communication. This book is not a condensed outline of all aspects of Italian grammar. It is a series of hints to help you use more effectively and with greater versatility phrases and vocabulary that you have already learned.

*How to Study* Essential Italian Grammar

If you have already studied Italian in a conventional manner you can use this book as a refresher by glancing through all of it first and then selecting those areas on which you wish to concentrate.

If you have never studied Italian grammar, then the following suggestions will be helpful:

**1.** Master several hundred useful phrases and expressions such as you will find in any good phrase book. You will understand the suggestions contained in *Essential Italian Grammar* more easily after you have achieved this basic working knowledge of Italian. The purpose of this book is to enable you to gain greater fluency once you have learned phrases and expressions, not to teach you to construct sentences from rules and vocabulary.

**2.** Read through *Essential Italian Grammar* at least once in its entirety. Don't be concerned if anything is not immediately clear to you. What may appear discouragingly difficult at first will become easier as your studies progress. But the first reading is necessary to acquaint you with terms and concepts peculiar to Italian grammar. Learning what these terms and concepts are will help you to improve your comprehension of Italian and to use more freely the expressions you already know. As you use Italian and hear it spoken, many of its grammatical patterns will become familiar to you. *Essential Italian Grammar* helps you to discover these patterns so that you can use them.

**3.** Go back to this book periodically. Sections which seem difficult or of doubtful benefit at first, may prove extremely useful later.

**4.** For the most part, the book follows a logical order, taking the major divisions of grammar in sequence. You will do best to follow this order. However, some students learn best when they study to answer an immediate question or need (e.g. how to form the comparative; how to conjugate the verb "to be", etc.). If you are one of these students, turn to the section that interests you. But read through the entire section, rather than just an isolated part. Individual remarks, taken out of context, are easily misunderstood.

**5.** Examples are given for every rule. It is helpful to memorize these examples. If you learn every example in *Essential Italian Grammar*, together with its literal translation, you will have encountered the basic difficulties of Italian and studied models for their solution.

**6.** You cannot study Italian systematically without an understanding of its grammar, and the use and understanding of grammatical terms is as essential as a knowledge of certain mechanical terms when you learn to drive a car. If your knowledge of grammatical terms is weak read the Glossary of Grammatical Terms (page 111) and refer to it whenever necessary.

In every language there are many ways to express the same thought. Some constructions are simple, others more difficult. During your first experiments in communication, use a simple construction. Throughout *Essential Italian Grammar* you will find suggestions on how to avoid complicated constructions in favour of simpler ones. You may ultimately wish to master a more sophisticated way of expressing yourself. Be satisfied at first with the simplest.

As you begin to speak Italian you will become aware of the areas in which you need the most help in grammar. If you have no one with whom to speak, speak mentally to yourself. In the course of a day see how many of the simple thoughts you've expressed in English you are able to turn into Italian. This kind of experimental self-testing will give direction to your study of grammar. Remember that you are studying this course in Italian not to pass an examination or to receive a certificate but to communicate with others on a simple but useful level. *Essential Italian Grammar* is not the equivalent of a formal course of study at a university. Although it could serve as a supplement to such a course, its primary aim is to help the adult study on his own. Indeed, no self-study or academic course or series of courses is ever ideally suited to all students. You must rely on and be guided by your own rate of learning and your own requirements and interests. *Essential Italian Grammar* makes self-study easier.

If this or any other grammar tends to inhibit you in speaking Italian, or in using what you have learned through phrase books or conversation courses, curtail your study of grammar until you feel it will really assist rather than hinder your speaking. Your objective is speaking, and you *can* learn to speak a language without learning its grammar. But because of its systematic approach, grammar is a short-cut to language learning for those who feel at home with it. The fundamental purpose of *Essential Italian Grammar* is to help you by eliminating hit-or-miss memorization.

# Pronunciation

### A note for beginners and the self-taught

A good pronunciation of Italian cannot be acquired from a book alone. *All* beginners should have the help of a teacher, or any educated Italian, to impart the pronunciation of the Italian words on pages 16–17, and next that of the sentences on pages 19, 20 and 21. The learner must listen carefully and mimic the sounds of each word and each sentence until he can pronounce them to the satisfaction of the teacher or native speaker. Repetition will be necessary in order to achieve this. The learner will note that every Italian word of more than one syllable has one vowel that must be particularly stressed. If he can pronounce all the words and phrases on the pages mentioned, even the self-taught learner should be able to proceed alone. It is desirable for all learners to have as much practise as possible with native speakers. Listening to Italian on the radio helps to accustom all learners to the sounds of the language.

# Suggestions for Vocabulary Building

**1.** Study words and word lists that answer real and preferably immediate personal needs. If you are planning to travel in the near future your needs are clear cut, and a good travel phrase book will provide you with the material you want. But select from this material what specifically applies to your case. For instance, if you don't plan to drive, don't spend time studying the parts of the car. If you like foreign foods, study the appropriate section of your phrase book. Even if you do not plan to travel in the near future, you will probably learn more quickly by imagining a travel situation.

**2.** Memorize by association. Phrase books usually give associated word lists. If you use a dictionary don't memorize words haphazardly but choose words which are related and belong to the same family.

**3.** Study the specialized vocabulary of your profession, business or hobby. If you are interested in real estate, learn the terms associated with property, buying, selling, leasing, etc. If you are interested in mathematics, acquire a vocabulary in this science. Many of these specialized words can be used in other areas too. You may not find specialized vocabularies in ordinary phrase books, but a good dictionary will help you to make up a list for your own use.

## Similarities between English and Italian Vocabulary

It will help you to expand your Italian vocabulary if you remember that many Italian words are similar in appearance and meaning to English words. Notice: *la radio* (the radio), *la professione* (the profession), *la medicina* (the medicine), *il telefono* (the telephone), *il teatro* (the theatre), *politico* (political).

Here are some common differences in spelling between English and Italian:

| English *k* or *ck* = Italian *c* or *cc* | | | | par*k*—par*c*o; sa*ck*—sa*cc*o |
|---|---|---|---|---|
| „ | *ph* | „ | *f* | *ph*rase–*f*rase; tele*ph*one—tele*f*ono |
| „ | *x* | „ | *s* or *ss* | fi*x*ed—fi*ss*o; e*x*ercise—e*s*ercizio |
| „ | *th* | „ | *t* | *th*eatre—*t*eatro |
| „ | *c* | „ | *z* or *zz* | for*c*e—for*z*a; ra*c*e—ra*zz*a |
| „ | *y* | „ | *i* | st*y*le—st*i*le |
| „ | *ou* | „ | *o* | c*ou*rt—c*o*rte |
| „ | *tion* | „ | *zione* | conversa*tion*—conversa*zione* |
| „ | *ous* | „ | *oso* | fam*ous*—fam*oso* |

Study this list of words, observing the differences between English and Italian:

| ENGLISH | ITALIAN |
|---|---|
| automobile | automobile |
| hotel | hotel |
| area | area |
| gas | gas |
| idea | idea |
| radio | radio |
| colour | colore |
| annual | annuale |

| | |
|---|---|
| commercial | commerciale |
| special | speciale |
| list | lista |
| problem | problema |
| person | persona |
| cost | costo |
| moment | momento |
| cause | causa |
| figure | figura |
| medicine | medicina |
| rose | rosa |
| minute | minuto |
| use | uso |
| tube | tubo |
| generous | generoso |
| delicious | delizioso |
| famous | famoso |
| precious | prezioso |
| philosophy | filosofia |
| geography | geografia |
| history | storia |
| nation | nazione |
| action | azione |
| collection | collezione |

# Word Order

Word order in Italian is frequently the same as in English. This, added to the similarities between many English and Italian words, often makes it easy to understand an Italian sentence even with a minimum knowledge of grammar. Compare the following sentences in Italian and in English:

Roma è la capitale d'Italia.
Rome is the capital of Italy.

I turisti visitano musei, teatri e monumenti.
The tourists visit museums, theatres and monuments.

# How to Form Questions

You can turn a simple statement into a question in one of the following three ways:

**1.** Leave the sentence as it is and simply add a question mark at the end. When speaking, raise your voice at the end of the sentence. This is often done in English too.

Mio padre è arrivato?
My father has arrived?

Lei parla inglese?
You speak English?

**2.** Invert the normal order of subject and predicate * and place the predicate before the subject.

È arrivato mio padre?
[Has arrived my father?]
Has my father arrived?

Parla inglese Lei?
[Speak English you?]
Do† you speak English?
È la capitale d'Italia Roma?
[Is the capital of Italy Rome?]
Is Rome the capital of Italy?

---

\* If you are not familiar with the terms and concepts used in grammar, turn now to the Glossary of Grammatical Terms at the end of the book.

† The verb "to do"—used in English questions such as "*Do* you want some coffee?"—is not used in this way in Italian.

**3.** Leave the sentence as it is and simply add *non è vero?* [not is true?] at the end. *Non è vero?* is the Italian equivalent of such English phrases as "isn't it?" "don't you?" "aren't you?" etc.

> Suo padre parla inglese, *non è vero?*
> Your father speaks English, *doesn't he?*

> Il primo capitolo è lungo, *non è vero?*
> The first chapter is long, *isn't it?*

### Interrogative Words

Most questions, in Italian, as in English, begin with a question word such as "when?" "where?" "who?" Study the following list carefully:

| *Come* | How | *Come* si dice in italiano? [How itself (it) says in Italian?] *How* do you say (this) in Italian? |
|--------|-----|-----------------------------------------------------------------------------------------------------|
| *Quando* | When | *Quando* parte l'ultimo treno? [When leaves the last train?] *When* does the last train leave? |
| *Dove* | Where | *Dove* siamo? [Where we are?] *Where* are we? |
| *Chi* | Who | *Chi* viene con noi? *Who* comes with us? |
| *Di chi* | Whose | *Di chi* è questa valigia? [Of whom is this suitcase?] *Whose* suitcase is this? |

| | | |
|---|---|---|
| *Quale* | Which | *Quale* preferisce Lei? |
| | | [Which prefer you?] |
| | | *Which* do you prefer? |
| *Che, Che cosa* | What | *Che* desidera? *Che cosa* desidera? |
| | | [What you wish? What thing you wish?] |
| | | *What* do you wish? |
| *Perchè* | Why | *Perchè* viaggia Lei? |
| | | [Why travel you?] |
| | | *Why* do you travel? |
| *Quanto* | How much | *Quanto* costa? |
| | | [How much costs?] |
| | | *How much* does it cost? |
| *Quanti* | How many | *Quanti* sono venuti? |
| | | [How many are come?] |
| | | *How many* have come? |

# Nouns and Articles

## Gender of Italian Nouns

All Italian nouns are either masculine or feminine. In general, nouns denoting male persons or animals are masculine, and nouns denoting female persons or animals are feminine. This rule, however, cannot be used as a guide for identifying the gender of the countless nouns which do not denote persons or animals. The best way to learn the gender of nouns is to memorize the definite article together with the noun.

## The Definite Article

In Italian the definite article agrees in gender and number with the noun it accompanies. English is simpler in this respect, for the same form, "the", is used for all nouns, singular or plural. The forms of the definite article in Italian are:

| MASC. SING. | MASC. PL. |
|:---:|:---:|
| *il* | *i* |
| *lo* | *gli* |
| *l'* | *gl'* |

| FEM. SING. | FEM. PL. |
|:---:|:---:|
| *la* | *le* |
| *l'* | *le* |

Observations on the definite article:

*Il* and *i*, *la* and *le* are the most common forms of the definite article.

*Lo* and *gli* are used before masculine nouns beginning with *z*, or with *s* followed by a consonant: *lo* zio (the uncle), *lo* sbaglio (the mistake).

*Gli* is also used before masculine plurals beginning with a vowel: *gli* anni (the years).

*Gl'* is used before masculine plurals beginning with *i*: *gl'*italiani (the Italians).

*L'* is used before singular nouns, masculine and feminine, beginning with a vowel: *l'*anno (the year), *l'*opera (the opera).

Study the following table carefully:

|  | SING. | | PL. | |
|---|---|---|---|---|
| MASC. | *il* | *il* signore, the gentle-man | *i* | *i* signori, the gentle-men |
| | *lo* | *lo* zio, the uncle | *gli* | *gli* zii, the uncles |
| | | *lo* sbaglio, the mistake | | *gli* sbagli, the mistakes |
| | *l'* | *l'*anno, the year | | *gli* anni, the years |
| | | | *gl'* | *gl'*italiani, the Italians |
| FEM. | *la* | *la* signora, the lady | *le* | *le* signore, the ladies |
| | *l'* | *l'*italiana, the Italian woman | | *le* italiane, the Italian women |
| | | | | *le* entrate, the en-trances |

## Plurals of Nouns

The majority of masculine nouns end in *-o* in the singular and change this *-o* to *-i* in the plural: il teatr*o* (the theatre), i teatr*i* (the theatres).

The majority of feminine nouns end in -*a* in the singular and change this -*a* to -*e* in the plural: la donn*a* (the woman), le donn*e* (the women).

Nouns which end in -*e* in the singular may be either masculine or feminine. These nouns change the -*e* to -*i* in the plural: la madr*e* (the mother), le madr*i* (the mothers); il padr*e* (the father), i padr*i* (the fathers).

There are a number of masculine nouns which end in -*a* in the singular. They change the -*a* to -*i* in the plural: il poet*a* (the poet), i poet*i* (the poets).

|  | SING. | PL. |  |
|---|---|---|---|
| feminine nouns ending in | -*a* ...... | -*e* | la donn*a*, le donn*e* |
| masculine nouns ending in -*o* | | | il libr*o*, i libr*i* |
| masculine nouns ending in -*a* | | -*i* | il poet*a*, i poet*i* |
| masculine nouns ending in -*e* | | | il padr*e*, i padr*i* |
| feminine nouns ending in -*e* | | | la madr*e*, le madr*i* |

### Irregularities in Noun Plurals

**1.** A number of masculine nouns ending in -*o* in the singular become feminine in the plural and have an irregular plural ending in -*a*. The most common of these nouns are:

| SING. | PL. |
|---|---|
| l'uov*o* (the egg) | le uov*a* (the eggs) |
| il bracci*o* (the arm) | le bracci*a* (the arms) |
| il dit*o* (the finger) | le dit*a* (the fingers) |
| il lenzuol*o* (the sheet) | le lenzuol*a* (the sheets) |
| il pai*o* (the pair) | le pai*a* (the pairs) |

**2.** Nouns ending in *-io* are of two kinds:

    (*a*) When the *i* of *-io* is stressed, the *-o* is changed to *-i*:
        lo *zio* (the uncle), gli *zii* (the uncles)

    (*b*) When the *i* of *-io* is not stressed, it drops out before
        the *-o* is changed to *-i*:
        il figl*io* (the son), i figl*i* (the sons)

**3.** (*a*) Nouns ending in *-co* and *-go* may or may not insert an *h* before changing the *-o* to *-i*. There is no simple general rule for this.

| SING. | PL. |
| --- | --- |
| il medic*o* (the doctor) | i medic*i* (the doctors) |
| l'amic*o* (the friend) | gli amic*i* (the friends) |
| il fuoc*o* (the fire) | i fuoc*hi* (the fires) |
| il fisiolog*o* (the physiologist) | i fisiolog*i* (the physiologists) |
| il lag*o* (the lake) | i lag*hi* (the lakes) |

(*b*) Nouns ending in *-ca* and *-ga* insert an *h* before changing the *-a* to *-e*.

| l'amic*a* (the friend) | le amic*he* (the friends) |
| --- | --- |
| la pag*a* (the salary) | le pag*he* (the salaries) |

**4.** Nouns ending in an accented vowel do not change in the plural: la citt*à* (the city), le citt*à* (the cities).

**5.** *L'uomo* (the man) has an irregular plural, *gli uomini* (the men).

## Noun Suffixes

A special feature of Italian nouns is that their meaning can be modified by the addition of suffixes. Thus, *ragazzo* (boy) can become *ragazzino* or *ragazzetto* (little boy), *ragazzone* (big, overgrown boy) and *ragazzaccio* (brat, nasty boy). *Casa* (house) can become *casetta* (little house), *libro* (book) can become *libriccino* (little book). The use of these and other suffixes is very frequent in idiomatic Italian, and it is well for you to be aware of it, even if you do not make use of suffixes yourself.

## Hints on the Identification of Gender

We have already said that the best way for you to remember the gender of a noun is to memorize the noun together with its article. There are, however, a few general rules which can help you in recognizing and remembering the gender of a noun.

**1.** You can recognize the gender of a noun by its ending.

(*a*) Masculine nouns generally end in -*o*: *il figlio* (the son).
(*b*) Feminine nouns generally end in -*a*: *la donna* (the woman).

Exceptions: *la mano* (the hand), *il poeta* (the poet), *il programma* (the programme) and a number of others.

**2.** The gender of a noun may be recognized by its meaning.

MASCULINE

(*a*) The names of male persons and animals are almost always masculine: *il padre* (the father), *il leone* (the lion).

(b) The names of the months and of the days of the week (except Sunday) are masculine: *il settembre* (September), *il lunedì* (Monday).

(c) The names of mountains and lakes are masculine: *il Vesuvio* (Vesuvius), *il Garda* (Lake Garda).

FEMININE

(d) The names of female persons and animals are usually feminine: *la madre* (the mother), *la leonessa* (the lioness).

(e) Abstract nouns of quality ending in an accented syllable are feminine: *la libertà* (liberty), *la virtù* (virtue).

(f) Names of almost all fruits are feminine: *la pera* (the pear), *la mela* (the apple).

## Masculine and Feminine Forms of the Same Noun

You can enlarge your vocabulary by observing the following changes in nouns:

(1) Changing the final vowel can make a masculine noun feminine:

Francesc*o* (Francis)—Francesc*a* (Frances)
figli*o* (son)—figli*a* (daughter)
sart*o* (tailor)—sart*a* (seamstress)
infermier*e* (male nurse)—infermier*a* (nurse)
padron*e* (boss, owner)—padron*a* (boss's wife, owner)

(2) Dropping the final vowel and adding a suffix can make a masculine noun feminine:

poeta (poet)—poet*essa* (poetess)
studente (student, masc.)—student*essa* (student, fem.)

(3) Some nouns refer to both male and female persons and adjust their gender accordingly:

> *il* nipote (the nephew)—*la* nipote (the niece)
> *il* cantante (the singer, masc.)—*la* cantante (the singer, fem.)

## Common Prepositions and the Definite Article

The most common Italian prepositions when used together with the definite article are contracted as follows:

| PREPOSITION | | | | DEFINITE ARTICLE | | | | |
|---|---|---|---|---|---|---|---|---|
| | | SINGULAR | | | | PLURAL | | |
| | *il* | *lo* | *la* | *l'* | *i* | *gli* | *gl'* | *le* |
| *a*, to, at | al | allo | alla | all' | ai | agli | agl' | alle |
| *da*, from, by | dal | dallo | dalla | dall' | dai | dagli | dagl' | dalle |
| *di*, of | del | dello | della | dell' | dei | degli | degl' | delle |
| *in*, in | nel | nello | nella | nell' | nei | negli | negl' | nelle |
| *su*, on | sul | sullo | sulla | sull' | sui | sugli | sugl' | sulle |
| *con*, with | col | No contractions with other forms of the definite article. | | | | | | |
| *per*, for | Does not contract at all. | | | | | | | |

Determine first what the proper form of the definite article is and then use the contracted form that corresponds to it.

> Non ci sono posti liberi *nella* sala da pranzo.
> [Not there are places free *in the* room for dining.]
> There are no empty places *in the* dining-room.

> Il prezzo *del* biglietto è seicento lire.
> The price *of the* ticket is 600 lire.

> Cerco un regalo *per il* compleanno di mia figlia.
> [I seek a gift *for the* birthday of my daughter.]
> I am looking for a gift for my daughter's birthday.

> Andremo *all'*opera *con gli* altri.
> We shall go *to the* opera *with the* others.

## The Indefinite Article

In English the indefinite article "a" becomes "an" when it precedes a vowel. In Italian, the indefinite article agrees in gender with the noun it accompanies.

Study the following table:

MASC.   *un*     *un* signore (a gentleman); *un* attore (an actor)

*uno*    *uno* zio (an uncle)

FEM.   *una*    *una* cugina (a (girl) cousin)

*un'*    *un'*amica (a (girl) friend)

Observations on the indefinite article:

*Un* is the usual form of the indefinite article used before a masculine noun; *una* is the usual form used before a feminine noun.

*Uno* is used before masculine nouns beginning with *z*, or with *s* followed by a consonant: *uno* zero (a zero), *uno* sbaglio (a mistake).

*Un'* is used before all feminine nouns beginning with a vowel: *un'*italiana (an Italian woman).

The indefinite article has no plural. To express an indefinite plural ("some") use the preposition *di* with the definite article: *dei* ragazzi (some boys), *delle* donne (some women).

# Adjectives

## Agreement of Adjectives with Nouns

In Italian adjectives agree in gender and number with the nouns they accompany. A masculine singular noun requires a masculine singular adjective, a feminine singular noun a feminine singular adjective, etc. In English the use of adjectives is simpler because they are invariable: a *red* house, two *red* houses.

## Forms of Adjectives

There are two kinds of adjectives in Italian: those which end in *-o* in the masculine singular, and those which end in *-e* in both the masculine and feminine singular.

**1.** Adjectives ending in *-o*:

|  | SING. | PL. |
|---|---|---|
| MASC. | italian*o* (Italian) | italian*i* (Italian) |
|  | ross*o* (red) | ross*i* (red) |
| FEM. | italian*a* (Italian) | italian*e* (Italian) |
|  | ross*a* (red) | ross*e* (red) |

**2.** Adjectives ending in *-e*:

|  | SING. | PL. |
|---|---|---|
| MASC. | ingles*e* (English) | ingles*i* (English) |
|  | cortes*e* (polite) | cortes*i* (polite) |
| FEM. | ingles*e* (English) | ingles*i* (English) |
|  | cortes*e* (polite) | cortes*i* (polite) |

| | |
|---|---|
| l'uomo italiano | the Italian man |
| gli uomini italiani | the Italian men |
| la donna italiana | the Italian woman |
| le donne italiane | the Italian women |
| l'uomo inglese | the English man |
| la donna inglese | the English woman |
| gli uomini inglesi | the English men |
| le donne inglesi | the English women |

Observations on adjectives:

Adjectives like *italiano* have four different endings (italiano, italiana, italiani, italiane).

Adjectives like *cortese* have only two different endings (cortese, cortesi).

## Position of Adjectives

In Italian the adjective usually follows the noun:

una parola *cortese*, a *polite* word
un lenzuolo *bianco*, a *white* sheet
una lingua *difficile*, a *difficult* language
dei viaggi *lunghi*,\* some *long* trips

A number of very common adjectives, however, often precede the noun in Italian, as in English:

| | |
|---|---|
| *bello*, beautiful, handsome, fine | una *bella* ragazza (a *good-looking* girl) |
| *buono*, good | *buone* notizie (*good* news) |

\* Adjectives ending in -*co* and -*go* may or may not retain the hard sound of the *c* or *g* in the plural: *bianco, bianca, bianchi, bianche* (white), but *greco, greca, greci, greche* (Greek).

| | |
|---|---|
| *nuovo*, new | un *nuovo* ristorante (a *new* restaurant) |
| *vecchio*, old | un *vecchio* amico (an *old* friend) |
| *piccolo*, small | un *piccolo* regalo (a *small* gift) |
| *grande*, big, large | una *grande* città (a *big* city) |
| *lungo*, long | una *lunga* strada (a *long* road) |
| *breve*, short | un *breve* soggiorno (a *short* stay) |
| *giovane*, young | un *giovane* ragazzo (a *young* boy) |
| *antico*, ancient | nell'*antico* palazzo (in the *ancient* palace) |
| *primo, secondo*, etc., first, second, etc. | la *prima* fermata (the *first* stop) |
| | la *seconda* colazione (lunch) [the *second* breakfast] |

Observation on the adjectives just listed:

**1.** The meaning of an adjective may change according to its position.  Compare:

| | |
|---|---|
| il ragazzo *povero* | the *poor* boy (not rich) |
| il *povero* ragazzo | the *poor* boy (unfortunate) |
| l'amico *vecchio* | the *aged* friend |
| il *vecchio* amico | the *old* friend (of long standing) |

In general, the adjective has its literal meaning when it follows the noun and a figurative meaning when it precedes it.

**2.** Adjectives which normally precede the noun may be placed after it for special emphasis:

Che viaggio *lungo*!     What a *long* journey!

## Special Forms of *bello, buono, grande*

When *bello, buono* and *grande* are placed immediately before their noun special forms are used. In all other cases these adjectives have their normal endings. Compare:

È un *buon* ristorante?
[Is a good restaurant?]
Is it a *good* restaurant?

Questo ristorante è *buono.*
This restaurant is *good.*

È *buono* questo ristorante?
[Is good this restaurant?]
Is this restaurant *good?*

### Bello

The special forms of *bello* are similar to the contractions formed by the prepositions *di* and *in* when used with the definite article.

|       | SING. | PL.   |                                                                      |
| ----- | ----- | ----- | -------------------------------------------------------------------- |
| MASC. | bel   | bei   | *bel* ragazzo, *bei* ragazzi<br>*handsome* boy, *handsome* boys       |
|       | bello | begli | *bello* scaffale, *begli* scaffali<br>*fine* bookcase, *fine* bookcases |
|       | bell' | begl' | *bell'*insetto, *begl'*insetti<br>*pretty* insect, *pretty* insects   |
| FEM.  | bella | belle | *bella* ragazza, *belle* ragazze<br>*lovely* girl, *lovely* girls     |
|       | bell' | belle | *bell'*automobile, *belle* entrate<br>*fine* car, *handsome* entrances |

Observation:

> *Begl'*, masculine plural, is used only before a noun beginning with *i-*.

## Buono

The special forms of *buono* in the singular are similar to the forms of the indefinite article.

|  | SING. | PL. |  |
|---|---|---|---|
| MASC. | buon | buoni | *buon* posto, *buoni* posti<br>*good* seat, *good* seats |
|  |  |  | *buon* attore, *buoni* attori<br>*good* actor, *good* actors |
|  | buono | buoni | *buono* zio, *buoni* zii<br>*good* uncle, *good* uncles |
| FEM. | buona | buone | *buona* madre, *buone* madri<br>*good* mother, *good* mothers |
|  | buon' |  | *buon'*analisi<br>*good* analysis |

## Grande

*Grande* becomes *gran* before a singular noun beginning with any consonant except *z* or *s* followed by a consonant: un *gran* libro (a good book), una *gran* donna (a wonderful woman), un *gran* pittore (a good painter). *Grand'* is the form used before a noun beginning with a vowel: un *grand'*uomo (a great man). The full form *grande* is also used in these cases for the sake of greater emphasis: un *grande* pittore (a great painter).

# Adverbs

In English adverbs are often formed by adding *-ly* to the adjective: clear, clear*ly*; recent, recent*ly*. In Italian adverbs are formed in a similar way, by adding *-mente* to the feminine singular of the adjective. Study this table:

| ADJECTIVE | | ADVERB |
|---|---|---|
| MASC. SING. | FEM. SING. | |
| assoluto (absolute) | assoluta | assoluta*mente* (absolutely) |
| chiaro (clear) | chiara | chiara*mente* (clearly) |
| rapido (rapid) | rapida | rapida*mente* (rapidly) |
| recente (recent) | recente | recente*mente* (recently) |

Lei parla troppo *rapidamente*.
You speak too quickly.

È *assolutamente* falso.
It is absolutely false.

Note that in adjectives ending in *-le* or *-re*, the final *-e* is dropped before adding *-mente*:

faci*le*, easy          facil*mente*, easily
regola*re*, regular     regolar*mente*, regularly

You should memorize the following list of common adverbs that do not end in *-mente*:

bene    well          Non mi sento *bene*.
                      [Not to me I feel well.]
                      I don't feel *well*.

| male | badly, poorly | Si sente *male*. |
| | | [To himself he feels badly.] |
| | | He feels *sick*. |
| troppo | too much | Costa *troppo*. |
| | | It costs *too much*. |
| molto | very, a lot | Mio padre è *molto* ricco. |
| | | My father is *very* rich. |
| assai | very | Andiamo *assai* lontano. |
| | | We are going *very* far. |
| tanto | so, so much, very much | Non *tanto*. |
| | | Not *so much*. |
| | | Egli canta *tanto* bene. |
| | | He sings *so* well. |
| adagio | slowly | Parli *adagio*, per favore. |
| | | Speak *slowly*, please. |
| presto | quickly, early | Venga *presto*. |
| | | Come *quickly*. |
| | | Ci alziamo sempre *presto*. |
| | | [Ourselves we get up always early.] |
| | | We always get up *early*. |
| sempre | always | Roma è *sempre* bella. |
| | | Rome is *always* beautiful. |
| subito | immediately | Partiamo *subito*. |
| | | We are leaving *immediately*. |
| spesso | often | Vado *spesso* a Roma. |
| | | I go *often* to Rome. |

# Comparisons of Adjectives and Adverbs

## Comparisons of Inequality

There are two ways of expressing comparison in English. You can add *-er* or *-est* to some adjectives and adverbs (sweet, sweet*er*, sweet*est*; soon, soon*er*, soon*est*). Or you can place the words "more" or "less", "most" or "least" before these and other adjectives and adverbs (beautiful, *more* or *less* beautiful, *most* or *least* beautiful; slowly, *more* or *less* slowly, *most* or *least* slowly).

In Italian there is only one way of expressing comparison. Place the words *più* (more), *il più* (most), or *meno* (less), *il meno* (least) before the adjective or adverb. In adjectives, the definite article in *il più* and *il meno* must agree with the noun.

Study the following table:

| | | |
|---|---|---|
| pesante, heavy | *più* pesante, heavier | *il più* pesante, heaviest |
| | *meno* pesante, less heavy | *il meno* pesante, least heavy |
| interessante, interesting | *più* interessante, more interesting | *il più* interessante, most interesting |
| | *meno* interessante, less interesting | *il meno* interessante, least interesting |

La mia valigia è pesante, ma la sua è *più* pesante. La valigia di mio marito è *la più* pesante.

My suitcase is heavy, but yours is heavier. My husband's suitcase is the heaviest.

È stato un viaggio interessante. Il viaggio di Pietro è stato *meno* interessante. Il viaggio di Mario *il meno* interessante di tutti.

It was an interesting trip. Peter's trip was less interesting. Mario's trip the least interesting of all.

Per favore, parli *più* lentamente, *il più* lentamente possibile. Please speak slowly, as slowly as possible.

## Irregular Comparative Forms

While most adjectives and adverbs express comparison regularly, some very common adjectives and adverbs have irregular forms of comparison which are used more frequently than the regular ones.

**ADJ.**

| | | |
|---|---|---|
| buono, good | più buono or *migliore*, better | il più buono or *il migliore*, best |
| cattivo, bad | più cattivo or *peggiore*, worse | il più cattivo or *il peggiore*, worst |
| grande, big | più grande or *maggiore*, larger, greater | il più grande or *il maggiore*, largest, greatest |

**ADV.**

| | | |
|---|---|---|
| bene, well | più bene or *meglio*, better | il più bene, or *il meglio*, best |
| male, badly | più male, or *peggio*, worse | il più male or *il peggio*, worst |

Questo è *il migliore* ristorante di * questa città.

* Note that the word "in" when used after a superlative is translated by *di* in Italian.

This is the best restaurant in this city.

Lei guida *peggio* di me.
She drives worse than I.

## The Absolute Superlative

Characteristic of Italian is the adjective or adverb which ends in *-issimo*. This form is called the absolute superlative because it implies no comparison. A similar absolute judgment is expressed in English when you say *very rich* or *extremely rich*, or when you use *excellent* instead of *the best*. Compare the meaning of "This book is excellent" with "This is the best book that I have read".

Add the suffix *-issimo* to the adjective or adverb after dropping the final vowel: povero (poor), pover*issimo* (extremely poor); male (badly), mal*issimo* (very badly); ricco (rich), ricch*issimo* (very rich).* For adverbs which end in *-mente*, the *-issimo* is added to the adjective before *-mente*: lento (slow), lent*issimo* (very slow), lent*issima*mente (very slowly). Remember that the form of the adjective to which *-mente* is added is the feminine singular: lentissim*a*.

È un'opera *interessantissima*.
It is a *very interesting* opera.

*Carissimo* amico!
My *very dear friend*!

Queste fragole sono *dolcissime*.
These strawberries are *very sweet*.

Lei parla *benissimo*.
You speak *extremely well*.

* For adjectives ending in *-co* or *-go* insert an *h* before adding *-issimo* to keep the hard sound of *c* or *g*: ricco (rich), ricc*h*issimo (very rich), lungo (long), lung*h*issimo (very long).

## The Word "than"

The word *than* used in comparisons (He is richer *than* you are) is translated by either *di* or *che* in Italian. An easy rule to remember is that *di* is used before *nouns, pronouns* and *numerals*, while *che* is used everywhere else. Observe the following examples:

Roma è più bella *di* Firenze. (noun)
Rome is more beautiful *than* Florence.

Mio padre è più ricco *di* me. (pronoun)
My father is richer *than* I.

Non voglio spendere più *di* mille lire. (numeral)
I don't want to spend more *than* 1,000 lire.

But:

Questa strada è più lunga *che* larga. (adjective)
This street is longer *than* (it is) wide.

È meglio partire subito *che* aspettare. (verb)
It is better to leave at once *than* to wait.

Parlo più spesso con lui *che* con suo fratello. (preposition)
I speak more often with him *than* with his brother.

### Comparisons of Equality

The "as . . . as" of comparisons of equality (I am *as* tall *as* my brother) is translated in Italian either by *così . . . come* or by *tanto . . . quanto*. As in English, the two words are placed around the adjective or adverb: *così* lungo *come* (*as long as*), *tanto* presto *quanto* (*as early as*). But contrary to English, the first term of the comparison, the *così* or the *tanto*, may be omitted without any change in meaning.

La nostra stanza è *così* cara *come* la loro.
La nostra stanza è cara *come* la loro.
Our room is *as* expensive *as* theirs.

Sono *tanto* ricco *quanto* lui.
Sono ricco *quanto* lui.
I am *as* rich *as* he.

# Expressing Possession

In English, you can say either "the teacher's book" or "the book of the teacher". There is no form corresponding to the apostrophe *s* in Italian. A form comparable to "the book of the teacher" is used.

le case *di* mio padre   il palazzo *del* re
[the houses *of* my father]   [the palace *of the* king]
my father's houses   the king's palace

## Possessive Adjectives

In Italian, the possessive adjective is almost always preceded by the definite article. Study the two words together as a unit.

| MASC. SING. | FEM. SING. | MASC. PL. | FEM. PL. | |
|---|---|---|---|---|
| il mio | la mia | i miei | le mie | my |
| il tuo | la tua | i tuoi | le tue | your (fam. sing.) |
| il suo | la sua | i suoi | le sue | his, her, its, your (polite sing.) |
| il nostro | la nostra | i nostri | le nostre | our |
| il vostro | la vostra | i vostri | le vostre | your (fam. sing. & pl.) |
| il loro | la loro | i loro | le loro | their, your (polite pl.) |

Observations on possessive adjectives:

**1.** The endings *-o, -a, -i, -e* are the same as those of other adjectives which end in *-o* in the masculine singular.

**2.** The masculine plural forms *i miei, i tuoi, i suoi* are irregular.

42

**3.** *Loro* is invariable.

**4.** Possessive adjectives agree in gender and number with the noun they accompany, that is, with the thing possessed:

> Dove sono *le nostre* valigie?
> Where are *our* suitcases?

> Signore, ecco *il suo* passaporto.
> Sir, here is *your* passport.

> Signora, ecco *il suo* passaporto.
> Madam, here is *your* passport.

> Ecco *i miei* fratelli e *le mie* sorelle.
> Here are *my* brothers and *my* sisters.

> Ecco *il suo* soprabito e *i suoi* guanti.
> Here is *your* overcoat and *your* gloves.

**5.** The definite article is omitted:

(*a*) before unmodified words of family relationship in the singular:

> *Mio* padre è vecchio.   *Sua* figlia è cortese.
> *My* father is old.   *His* daughter is polite.

(*b*) after the word *questo* and after numerals:

> *Questo* mio orologio si è fermato.
> [This my watch has stopped.]
> *This* watch of mine has stopped.

> *Due* miei amici non sono ancora arrivati.
> [Two my friends not have yet arrived.]
> *Two* friends of mine have not yet arrived.

(*c*) when the possessive stands alone:

> Di chi è questo libro? È *mio*.
> [Of whom is this book? Is mine.]
> Whose book is this? It's *mine*.
>
> Quel cane è *nostro*.
> That dog is *ours*.

**6.** Sometimes, contrary to English usage, the possessive adjective itself is omitted. This happens especially with parts of the body or with articles of clothing about whose ownership there can be no doubt. Then the definite article is used instead of the possessive adjective.

> Ho perduto *i* guanti.
> [I have lost *the* gloves.]
> I have lost *my* gloves.
>
> Ha perduto *la* testa.
> He lost *his* head.

# Demonstrative Adjectives and Pronouns

## Demonstrative Adjectives

The demonstrative adjectives *questo* (this) and *quello* (that) refer, as in English, to both persons and things. They always agree with the noun they accompany.

*Questo* has the four adjective endings *-o, -a, -i, -e*, with which you are already familiar. *Questo* and *questa* become *quest'* before a noun beginning with a vowel. *Questi* and *queste* may become *quest'* before plural nouns beginning with *i* and *e* respectively.

|       | SING.  | PL.    |                                                         |
|-------|--------|--------|---------------------------------------------------------|
| MASC. | questo | questi | *questo* fiore, *questi* fiori<br>this flower, these flowers |
|       | quest' |        | *quest'*albergo, *questi* alberghi<br>this hotel, these hotels |
| FEM.  | questa | queste | *questa* bambola, *queste* bambole<br>this doll, these dolls |
|       | quest' |        | *quest'*azione, *queste* azioni<br>this action, these actions |

*Quest'*individui amano cantare. These individuals like to sing.

Mi piace *quest'*aperitivo. I like this apéritif.
[To me is pleasing this apéritif.]

*Questa* ragazza balla bene. This girl dances well.
*Questo* treno è lento. This train is slow.

*Quello*, when it precedes its noun or adjective, has the same forms as *bello* when *bello* precedes the noun.

|  | SING. | PL. |  |
|---|---|---|---|
| MASC. | quel | quei | *Quel* ragazzo non è italiano. *That* boy is not Italian. *Quei* pacchi sono pesanti. *Those* packages are heavy. |
|  | quell' | quegli | Non abita più a *quell'*indirizzo. He no longer lives at *that* address. Non conosco *quegli* uomini. I don't know *those* men. |
|  | quello | quegli | *Quello* spettacolo comincia alle 4. *That* show begins at 4. *Quegli* studenti sono stranieri. *Those* students are foreigners. |
| FEM. | quella | quelle | *Quella* signora è americana. *That* lady is American. *Quelle* montagne sono alte. *Those* mountains are high. |
|  | quell' | quelle | *Quell'*automobile è bella. *That* car is beautiful. *Quelle* albicocche sono deliziose. *Those* apricots are delicious. |

Observation:

*Quegli* (MASC. PL.) becomes *quegl'* before a masculine plural noun beginning with *i*: *quegl'*italiani (those Italians).

## Questo and Quello as Pronouns

When used as pronouns, *questo* means "this" or "this one", *quello* "that" or "that one". They can refer to both persons and things. *Questi* (this one, this man) and *quegli* (that one, that man) are masculine singular pronouns which refer only to persons.

*Questo* mi piace più di *quello*.
[*This* to me is pleasing more than *that*.]
I like *this one* better than *that one*.

*Quello* che ha detto è vero.
[*That* which (he) has said is true.]
What he said is true.

Quali guanti preferisce sua moglie? *Quelli*.
Which gloves does your wife prefer? *Those*.

*Questi* non dice la verità.
*This man* does not tell the truth.

*Questi* è mio padre, *quegli* mio marito.
*This one* is my father, *that one* my husband.

## The Pronoun *ciò*

*Ciò* (this, that) is very often used instead of *questo* and *quello* to refer to things.

*Ciò* è falso.
This is false.

*Ciò* che ha detto è vero.
[That which (he) has said is true.]
What he said is true.

# Personal Pronouns

In Italian, as in English, pronouns have different forms according to their use and position in a sentence.

## Subject Pronouns

|            |       | SING.         |       | PL.          |
| ---------- | ----- | ------------- | ----- | ------------ |
| 1ST PERS.  | io    | I             | noi   | we           |
| 2ND PERS.  | tu    | you (fam.)    | voi   | you (fam.)   |
| 3RD PERS   | egli  | he            | loro  | they         |
|            | lui   | he            |       |              |
|            | lei   | she           |       |              |
|            | esso  | it (masc.)    | essi  | they (masc.) |
|            | essa  | it (fem.)     | esse  | they (fem.)  |
|            | Lei   | you (polite)  | Loro  | you (polite) |

Observations on subject pronouns:

**1.** The pronoun *ella* (she) is no longer in current use. *Esso* and *essa* with the meaning of "he" and "she" are also going out of use, and are replaced more and more frequently by *lui* and *lei*.

**2.** The Italian pronouns which translate the English "you" are *tu, voi, Lei* and *Loro*. Since *tu* is used in addressing members of the family and close friends, and *voi* in the singular has a somewhat condescending connotation, the tourist will probably use only *Lei* (sing.) and *Loro* (pl.). Concentrate on these forms.

**3.** Since Italian verbs have endings that indicate the person, it is not necessary to use the subject pronoun with verbs as in English.

> Viaggiamo spesso.     Fuma?
> We travel often.       Do you smoke?

**4.** The subject pronoun *io* is used when contrast or emphasis is involved.

> Parto domani mattina.
> I am leaving tomorrow morning.
>
> *Io* parto domani, ma mio fratello parte la settimana prossima.
> *I'm* leaving tomorrow, but my brother is leaving next week.

### Direct and Indirect Object Pronouns

In English the object pronouns (me, you, him, her, it, us, them) are either direct (He takes *it*) or indirect (He gives *me* the book, i.e. He gives the book *to me*). The same is true in Italian, except that in several cases object pronouns have a different form when they are direct and when they are indirect. Compare the two tables:

|        |            | DIRECT OBJECT PRONOUNS |                  | INDIRECT OBJECT PRONOUNS |
|--------|------------|------|------------------|------------------------|
| SING.  | 1st person | mi   | me               | mi (to) me             |
|        | 2nd person | ti   | you (familiar)   | ti (to) you (familiar) |
|        | 3rd person | lo   | him, it (masc.)  | gli (to) him, it (masc.) |
|        |            | la   | her, it (fem.)   | le (to) her, it (fem.) |
|        |            | La   | you (polite)     | Le (to) you (polite)   |

| | | DIRECT OBJECT PRONOUNS | | INDIRECT OBJECT PRONOUNS |
|---|---|---|---|---|
| PL. | 1st person | ci | us | ci (to) us |
| | 2nd person | vi | you (familiar) | vi (to) you (familiar) |
| | 3rd person | li | them (masc.) | loro (to) them (masc.) |
| | | le | them (fem.) | loro (to) them (fem.) |
| | | Li | you (polite) (masc.) | Loro (to) you (polite) (masc.) |
| | | Le | you (polite) (fem.) | Loro (to) you (polite) (fem.) |

*Ci* hanno dato questo libro. (indir. object)
They gave *us* this book.

*Mi* dica la verità. (indir. object)
Tell *me* the truth.

*Lo* conosco molto bene. (dir. object)
I know *him* very well.

Ora non *la* vedo, ma *le* ho parlato dieci minuti fa. (dir. object)
Now I don't see *her*, but I spoke *to her* ten minutes ago. (indir. object)

Observations:

**1.** Since you will probably use only *Lei* and *Loro* to translate the English "you", concentrate on the direct and indirect object pronouns which correspond to them: *La* (you) and *Le* (to you), *Li, Le* (you) and *Loro* (to you). These forms are often capitalized in writing to distinguish them from *la* (her), *le* (to her), *li, le* (them) and *loro* (to them).

Non *Le* possiamo dare questa lettera.
We can't give *you* this letter.

**2.** Object pronouns, with the exception of *loro*, precede the verb.

*Li* abbiamo visti e abbiamo parlato *loro*.
We saw *them* and we spoke *to them*.

**3.** But if the verb is an infinitive or a participle the pronoun follows it and is written as one word with it. The final *-e* of the infinitive is dropped before adding a pronoun. *Loro* always stands alone.

Voglio sentir*lo*.
I want to hear *it*.

Vedendo*lo*, *lo* riconobbi.
Seeing *him*, I recognized *him*.

Voglio dare *loro* il libro.
I want to give *them* the book.

**4.** The object pronoun also follows the verb and is written as one word with it in an affirmative command, but *not* with commands given to persons addressed as *Lei* and *Loro*.

Dite*mi* la verità. (voi)
Tell *me* the truth.

*Mi* dica la verità. (Lei)
Tell *me* the truth.

**5.** *Lo* and *la* become *l'* before a verb beginning with a vowel or with *h*.

*L'*accettiamo volentieri.
We accept *it* gladly.

*L'*ho visto ieri.
I saw *him* yesterday.

### Direct and Indirect Object Pronouns with the Same Verb

When a verb has both a direct and an indirect object pronoun the indirect precedes the direct. Note that the *i* of *mi*, *ti*, *ci* and *vi* changes to *e* before *lo*, *la*, *li* and *le*. *Gli* and *le* both become *glie* before *lo*, *la*, *li* and *le*. The *glie* and the pronoun following it are written as one word.

*Me lo* dice.
He tells *it to me*.

*Glieli* vendo con piacere.
I sell *them to you* (or to him, or to her) with pleasure.

### Stressed Forms of the Personal Pronouns

These are the pronouns used after prepositions:

| SING. | | PL. | |
|---|---|---|---|
| per *me* | for *me* | fra di *noi* | among *us* |
| con *te* | with *you* (fam. sing.) | prima di *voi* | before *you* (fam. pl.) |
| di *lui* | of *him* | vicino a *loro* | near *them* (masc. & fem.) |
| con *lei* | with *her* | | |
| a *Lei* | to *you* (polite sing.) | a *Loro* | to *you* (polite pl.) |

### How to Avoid the Use of Double Pronouns

You can avoid object pronouns (I gave *it* to *him*) by replacing them with nouns (I gave *the book* to *John*). You can avoid using two pronouns with the same verb by replacing one of them with a noun (I gave *it* to *John*).

*Me lo* diede. (2 obj. pro.)    *Mi* diede il libro. (1 obj. pro.)
He gave *it to me*.            He gave *me* the book.

*Gliela* mostrai. (2 obj. pro.)    *Gli* mostrai la casa. (1 obj.
I showed *it to him*.              pro.)
                                    I showed *him* the house.

Instead of the indirect object pronoun you can use the stressed form of the pronoun with the preposition *a* (to). In this way you avoid combinations such as *glielo, me lo*, etc.

*Me lo* diede.              *Lo* diede *a me*.
He gave *it to me*.       He gave *it to me*.

*Gliela* mostrai.          *La* mostrai *a lui*.
I showed *it to him*.      I showed *it to him*.

## Table of Personal Pronouns

You will find the following tables useful in reviewing the personal pronouns. For the sake of completeness we are including the *reflexive pronouns* here too. You will need to know them when you study reflexive verbs on page 95.

The second table, on page 55, illustrates the changes in personal pronouns which occur when there is both a direct and an indirect object pronoun used with the same verb.

## TABLE OF PRONOUNS

|  | UNSTRESSED | | | | STRESSED | |
|  | SUBJECT | | OBJECT | | REFLEXIVE | |
|  | | | DIRECT | INDIRECT | | |
|---|---|---|---|---|---|---|
| SING. | | | | | | |
| 1st person | io | I | mi me | mi to me | mi myself, to myself | me me |
| 2nd person | tu | you (fam.) | ti you | ti to you | ti yourself, to yourself | te you |
| 3rd person | egli, lui | he | lo him, it | gli to him, it | si himself, herself, itself, to himself, etc. | lui him |
| | lei | she | la her, it | le to her, it | | lei her |
| | esso | it (masc.) | | | | esso it |
| | essa | it (fem.) | | | | essa it |
| | | | | | | se himself, herself, itself |
| | Lei | you (polite) | La you | Le to you | si yourself, to yourself | Lei you |
| | | | | | | se yourself |

|  | SUBJECT | | OBJECT | | | | REFLEXIVE | | STRESSED | |
| --- | --- | --- | --- | --- | --- | --- | --- | --- | --- | --- |
|  | | | DIRECT | | INDIRECT | | | | | |
| **PL.** | | | | | | | | | | |
| 1st person | noi | we | ci | us | ci | to us | ci | ourselves, to ourselves | noi | us |
| 2nd person | voi | you (fam.) | vi | you | vi | to you | vi | yourself, yourselves, to yourself, etc. | voi | you |
| 3rd person | loro | they | li | them | loro | to them | si | themselves, to themselves | loro | them |
|  | essi | they (masc.) | le | them | | | | | essi | them |
|  | esse | they (fem.) | | | | | | | esse | them |
|  | | | | | | | | | se | themselves |
|  | Loro | you (polite) | Li | you | Loro | to you | si | yourselves, to yourselves | Loro | you |
|  | | | Le | you | | | | | se | yourselves |

## Relative Position of Pronouns

When a direct and an indirect pronoun are used together the indirect precedes the direct and undergoes the following changes:

| | | | | |
|---|---|---|---|---|
| me lo | me la | me li | me le | him, her, it, them to me |
| te lo | te la | te li | te le | him, her, it, them to you (fam. sing.) |
| glielo | gliela | glieli | gliele | him, her, it, them to him, her, it, you (pol. sing.) |
| se lo | se la | se li | se le | him, her, it, them to himself, herself, itself, yourself (pol.) |
| ce lo | ce la | ce li | ce le | him, her, it, them to us |
| ve lo | ve la | ve li | ve le | him, her, it, them to you (fam. pl.) |
| se lo | se la | se li | se le | him, her, it, them to themselves, yourselves (pol.) |

The indirect pronoun *loro* (*Loro*) is always placed after the verb:

> Egli lo (la, li, le) dà *loro*.
> He gives him (her, them, etc.) *to them*.

> Egli lo dà *Loro*.
> He gives it *to you* (pol. pl.).

# Negatives

In Italian any sentence can be made negative by placing *non* (not) before the verb.

Questa città *non* è molto grande.
This city is *not* very large.

*Non* parlo molto bene.
[Not I speak very well.]
I do *not* speak very well.

If there is an object pronoun preceding the verb, *non* is placed before the pronoun and not directly before the verb.

*Non* lo vedo.
[*Not* him I see.]
I don't see him.

*Non* mi può chiamare un tassì?
[*Not* to me can call a taxi?]
Can't you call me a taxi?

Other important negatives are:

| | |
|---|---|
| non . . . mai | never |
| non . . . più | no longer |
| non . . . niente | nothing |
| non . . . nessuno | nobody |
| non . . . neanche | not even |
| non . . . nè . . . nè | neither . . . nor |

*Non* sono *mai* stato in Italia.
[*Not* am *ever* been in Italy.]
I have *never* been in Italy.

*Non* vedo *niente.*
[*Not* I see *nothing.*]
I see *nothing.*

*Non* è venuto *nessuno.*
[*Not* is come *nobody.*]
*Nobody* came.

*Non* abita *più* qui.
[*Not* he lives *more* here.]
He *no longer* lives here.

*Non* è venuto *neanche* il presidente.
[*Not* is come *not even* the president.]
*Not even* the president came.

*Non* abbiamo visitato *nè* Roma *nè* Firenze.
[*Not* we have visited *neither* Rome *nor* Florence.]
We visited *neither* Rome *nor* Florence.

Observations:

Negative words, such as *niente* (nothing), *mai* (never), etc., are almost always used with *non*. *Non* is placed before the verb, the other negative word after the verb.

Negative words may also stand alone, as in the sentence:

Chi è venuto con Lei? *Nessuno.*
Who came with you? *No one.*

# Che, Cui, Chi

## *Che* as Conjunction

In English the conjunction *that* is frequently omitted. (*I think that he will come* is often abbreviated to *I think he will come*.) In Italian the conjunction *che* must be expressed.

Credo *che* verrà.
I think (*that*) he will come.

Sa *che* non sono ancora arrivati?
Do you know (*that*) they haven't arrived yet?

## *Che* as Relative Pronoun

In addition to being a conjunction, *che* is also a relative pronoun (*who, which, that, whom*). It refers to either persons or things, and can be used as either subject or object. It is the most important of the relative pronouns.

È lo stesso cameriere *che* era qui ieri. (refers to a person, subject)
He is the same waiter *who* was here yesterday.

Ecco un vestito *che* non costa molto. (refers to a thing, subject)
Here is a dress *which* doesn't cost much.

L'uomo *che* cerca non abita più qui. (refers to a person, object)
The man *whom* you are looking for no longer lives here.

Non trovo il dizionario *che* ho comprato ieri. (refers to a thing, object)

I don't find the dictionary *which* I bought yesterday.

## The Relative Pronoun *Cui*

After prepositions a special form of the relative pronoun is used: *cui*. *Cui*, too, stands for either persons or things.

L'uomo *con cui* parlo è il direttore. (refers to a person)
The man *with whom* I am speaking is the director.

La porta *da cui* si esce è a sinistra. (refers to a thing)
The door *by which* one leaves is to the left.

## The Interrogative Pronoun *Chi*

*Che* is often confused with *chi*. Use *chi* as an interrogative to refer to persons.

*Chi* è quell'uomo?
*Who* is that man?

Con *chi* sei venuto?
With *whom* did you come?

# Conjunctions

Although we are emphasizing simple straightforward expressions, there will be need from time to time to use longer, more complicated sentences. For this purpose you should become acquainted with the following list of basic conjunctions:

| | | |
|---|---|---|
| *e* | and | Ho veduto questo quadro *e* l'ho comprato. |
| | | I saw this picture *and* I bought it. |
| *o* | or | Vuole andare al cinema *o* preferisce il teatro? |
| | | Do you want to go to the cinema *or* do you prefer the theatre? |
| *ma* | but | Vorrei comprarlo *ma* non ho denari con me. |
| | | I would like to buy it *but* I haven't got money with me. |
| *quando* | when | Partirò *quando* parte Lei. |
| | | I shall leave *when* you are leaving. |
| *mentre* | while | Io andrò a Roma *mentre* mio marito resta qui. |
| | | I shall go to Rome *while* my husband stays here. |
| *se* | if | Lo comprerò *se* mi piace. |
| | | I shall buy it *if* I like it. |

| | | |
|---|---|---|
| *perchè* | because | Prendo l'ombrello *perchè* piove. |
| | | I'm taking the umbrella *because* it's raining. |
| *benchè* | although (followed by subjunctive) | Uscirò *benchè* sia tardi. |
| | | I shall go out *although* it is late. |

# Verbs

Before proceeding to study this section, you should become acquainted with the material covered in pages 111–122 of the Glossary of Grammatical Terms. Although you may not remember everything at a first reading, this material will help you to understand special constructions and expressions as you come to them.

## Comparisons of English and Italian Verbs

Italian verbs are more complicated than English ones. In English there are very few changes in ending, and those that do occur are relatively uniform: I sing, he sing*s*; I take, he take*s*. In Italian, each person has its own distinctive ending: io parl*o* (*I* speak), tu parl*i* (*you* speak). Since the subject pronoun is very often omitted in Italian, failure to employ the correct ending results in misunderstanding: parl*o* (*I* speak), parl*a* (*he* speaks).

Another aspect in which Italian verbs are more complicated than English is the greater number of tenses used in Italian. You will notice this when we speak of the various past tenses and of the subjunctive mood. Though it is possible to avoid some difficulties by using short, simple sentences, it is necessary to be acquainted with the various aspects of the Italian verb for understanding the spoken and the written language. In the pages which follow, we shall always distinguish between those forms which must be memorized from the start and those which you can study at a later date.

## The Three Conjugations

All Italian verbs belong to one of three conjugations. Since the various endings which a particular verb takes are determined by the conjugation to which it belongs, you must pay special attention to this point. By classifying verbs into conjugations it is easier to remember their many forms.

The conjugation to which an Italian verb belongs is determined by the ending of its infinitive (that is, of the form which corresponds to the English "to walk", "to have", etc.).

Verbs ending in -*are* belong to the *first conjugation*
    ,,      ,,   ,, -*ere*   ,,    ,,  ,, *second conjugation*
    ,,      ,,   ,, -*ire*    ,,    ,,  ,, *third conjugation*

All verbs which belong to the same conjugation (except irregular ones) are conjugated like the model verb of that conjugation. Our model verbs are:

| | |
|---|---|
| *parlare* (to speak) | *first conjugation* |
| *vendere* (to sell) | *second conjugation* |
| *partire* (to depart) | *third conjugation* |
| *capire* (to understand) | *third conjugation* |

Regular verbs ending in -*are* will therefore take the same endings as the model verb *parlare*. Regular verbs in -*ere* and -*ire* will take the same endings as the models *vendere* and *partire* or *capire* respectively.

Irregular verbs will be treated separately, tense by tense.

## The Present Tense

### Comparison of Present Tense in English and Italian

In English we have three different ways of expressing an action in the present. We can say "I walk", "I am walking" or "I do walk". The three forms are distinguished by slight differences in meaning. In Italian, on the other hand, the present tense conveys all three meanings of the English.

### First Conjugation

Memorize the present tense of the model verb *parlare* (to speak):

| (io) | parl*o* | I speak, am speaking, do speak |
|------|---------|-------------------------------|
| (tu) | parl*i* | you (fam. sing.) speak, are speaking, do speak |
| (egli) | parl*a* | he (she, it) speaks, is speaking, does speak; you (polite, sing.) speak, are speaking, do speak |
| (noi) | parl*iamo* | we speak, are speaking, do speak |
| (voi) | parl*ate* | you (fam. pl., also sing.) speak, are speaking, do speak |
| (loro) | parl*ano* | they speak, are speaking, do speak; you (polite pl.) speak, are speaking, do speak |

### Second Conjugation

Memorize the present tense of the model verb *vendere* (to sell):

| (io) | vend*o* | I sell, am selling, do sell |
|------|---------|-----------------------------|
| (tu) | vend*i* | you (fam. sing.) sell, are selling, do sell |
| (egli) | vend*e* | he (she, it) sells, is selling, does sell; you (polite sing.) sell, are selling, do sell |
| (noi) | vend*iamo* | we sell, are selling, do sell |
| (voi) | vend*ete* | you (fam. pl., also sing.) sell, are selling, do sell |
| (loro) | vend*ono* | they sell, are selling, do sell; you (polite pl.) sell, are selling, do sell |

## Third Conjugation

Memorize the present tense of the model verb *partire* (to depart):

| | | |
|---|---|---|
| (io) | part*o* | I depart, am departing, do depart |
| (tu) | part*i* | you (fam. sing.) depart, are departing, do depart |
| (egli) | part*e* | he (she, it) departs, is departing, does depart; you (polite sing.) depart, are departing, do depart |
| (noi) | part*iamo* | we depart, are departing, do depart |
| (voi) | part*ite* | you (fam. pl., also sing.) depart, are departing, do depart |
| (loro) | part*ono* | they depart, are departing, do depart; you (polite, pl.) depart, are departing, do depart |

The third conjugation differs from the other two conjugations because not all its regular verbs follow the pattern of the model verb. The majority of third conjugation verbs insert the suffix *-isc-* before the ending in all persons of the singular and in the third person plural. There is no easy rule by which you can recognize which third conjugation verbs are like *partire* and which are like *capire* (to understand). When you learn new verbs try to remember to which category they belong.

Memorize the present tense of *capire* (to understand) as a model for third conjugation verbs of the second category:

| | | |
|---|---|---|
| (io) | cap*isco* | I understand, am understanding, do understand |
| (tu) | cap*isci* | you (fam. sing.) understand, do understand, are understanding |

| (egli) cap*isce* | he (she, it) understands, is understanding, does understand; you (polite sing.) understand, are understanding, do understand |
| (noi) cap*iamo* | we understand, are understanding, do understand |
| (voi) cap*ite* | you (fam. pl., also sing.) understand, are understanding, do understand |
| (loro) cap*iscono* | they understand, are understanding, do understand; you (polite pl.) understand, are understanding, do understand |

Observations on the present tense:

**1.** If you prefer, you may omit the second person singular form in memorizing, since you will not be likely to use it.

**2.** To help you remember the endings of the present tense for the three conjugations note that:

(*a*) in all three conjugations, the first person singular ends in -*o*; the second person singular in -*i*; the first person plural in -*iamo*.

(*b*) the second person plural ending has the characteristic vowel of the infinitive: parl*ate*, vend*ete*, cap*ite*, but is otherwise the same in all three conjugations.

(*c*) in the second and third conjugations, all endings are alike, except for the second person plural: vend*ete*, cap*ite*. The suffix -*isc*-, which appears in third conjugation verbs, does not technically count as an ending.

(*d*) in the first conjugation, you find the same vowel *a* in the third person, both singular and plural: parl*a*, parl*ano*.

## The Present Tense of Commonly Used Irregular Verbs

Some of the verbs most commonly used in Italian are not conjugated like the model verbs. They are irregular and must be memorized.

| Infinitive | io | tu | egli | noi | voi | loro |
|---|---|---|---|---|---|---|
| avere (to have) | ho | hai | ha | abbiamo | avete | hanno |
| essere (to be) | sono | sei | è | siamo | siete | sono |
| andare (to go) | vado | vai | va | andiamo | andate | vanno |
| dare (to give) | do | dai | dà | diamo | date | danno |
| *fare (to do) | faccio | fai | fa | facciamo | fate | fanno |
| stare (to be) | sto | stai | sta | stiamo | state | stanno |
| dovere (to have to) | devo | devi | deve | dobbiamo | dovete | devono |
| potere (to be able) | posso | puoi | può | possiamo | potete | possono |
| sapere (to know) | so | sai | sa | sappiamo | sapete | sanno |
| *bere (to drink) | bevo | bevi | beve | beviamo | bevete | bevono |
| tenere (to hold) | tengo | tieni | tiene | teniamo | tenete | tengono |
| *dire (to say, tell) | dico | dici | dice | diciamo | dite | dicono |
| venire (to come) | vengo | vieni | viene | veniamo | venite | vengono |
| *uscire (to go out) | esco | esci | esce | usciamo | uscite | escono |

## The Progressive Present

In studying the present tense in Italian you no doubt noticed that *parlo* was translated both as "I speak" and as "I am speaking". The form "I am speaking" is more vivid than "I speak" because the action is represented as going on, as being in progress. However, there is no time difference between the two forms, so that we can say either "The boat leaves" or "The boat is leaving" and refer to exactly the same time. Both in English and in Italian the present participle (the verb form ending in -*ing*: "taking", "looking") is used in forming the progressive.

* Some irregularities can be explained by keeping in mind that a number of verbs originally had another infinitive form: dire, dicere; fare, facere; uscire, escire; bere, bevere.

## The Present Participle

In Italian the present participle is formed by dropping the infinitive ending *-are*, *-ere*, *-ire*, and adding *-ando* to verbs of the first conjugation, *-endo* to verbs of the second and the third.

| | |
|---|---|
| compr*are* (to buy) | compr*ando* (buying) |
| vend*ere* (to sell) | vend*endo* (selling) |
| fin*ire* (to finish) | fin*endo* (finishing) |

## The Use of *Stare*

Of the two Italian verbs which mean "to be", the one which is used in forming the progressive is *stare*.*

| | |
|---|---|
| *Sto finendo* questa lettera. | *I am finishing* this letter. |
| Il piroscafo *sta partendo*. | The boat *is leaving*. |
| *Stiamo facendo* colazione. | *We are having* breakfast. |
| Che cosa *sta scrivendo*? | What *are you writing*? |
| A chi *sta scrivendo*? | To whom *are you writing*? |

## The Imperative or Command Form

To distinguish between the different verb forms used for giving commands, we must go back to the different pronouns which all mean "you" in Italian: *tu*, *Lei*, *voi*, *Loro*. Since you will be using the polite form (*Lei* and *Loro*) most frequently, we shall study that first. Concentrate on the singular.

* Other differences in the use of *essere* and *stare* will be discussed on page 106.

**Third Person Command Forms**

| | |
|---|---|
| *parlare* (to speak) | parl*i* (polite sing.)—speak!<br>parl*ino* (polite pl.)—speak! |
| *vedere* (to see) | ved*a* (polite sing.)—see!<br>ved*ano* (polite pl.)—see! |
| *partire* (to depart) | part*a* (polite sing.)—leave!<br>part*ano* (polite pl.)—leave! |
| *finire* (to finish) | finisc*a* (polite sing.)—finish!<br>finisc*ano* (polite pl.)—finish! |

Observe that those third conjugation verbs which insert -*isc*- in the present, do so in the command form as well.

Many of the more common verbs have irregular command forms for the polite singular and plural. Here are the most useful:

| | |
|---|---|
| *fare* (to do) | faccia (polite sing.)—do!<br>facciano (polite pl.)—do! |
| *andare* (to go) | vada (polite sing.)—go!<br>vadano (polite pl.)—go! |
| *dare* (to give) | dia (polite sing.)—give!<br>diano (polite pl.)—give! |
| *stare* (to be) | stia (polite sing.)—be!<br>stiano (polite pl.)—be! |
| *bere* (to drink) | beva (polite sing.)—drink!<br>bevano (polite pl.)—drink! |
| *dire* (to say) | dica (polite sing.)—say!<br>dicano (polite pl.)—say! |
| *tenere* (to hold, to take) | tenga (polite sing.)—take!<br>tengano (polite pl.)—take! |

To soften a command add the expressions *per favore* or *per piacere* ("please").

Apra la finestra, *per piacere.*
Open the window, please.

Mi porti un altro bicchiere, *per favore.*
Bring me another glass, please.

To avoid the command form altogether use the expressions *Mi faccia il piacere di* ("Do me the favour of") or *Vorrebbe* ("Would you") with the infinitive.

*Mi faccia il piacere* di aprire la finestra.
Please open the window.

*Vorrebbe* aprire la finestra, *per piacere?*
Would you please open the window?

*Mi faccia il piacere* di parlare più lentamente.
Please speak more slowly.

*Vorrebbe* parlare più lentamente, *per piacere?*
Would you please speak more slowly?

### First Person Plural Commands

The first person plural command ("Let's go!" "Let's sing!") is always the same as the present in Italian.

*Andiamo!* (Let's go!)     *Leggiamo!* (Let's read!)
*Cantiamo!* (Let's sing!)     *Corriamo!* (Let's run!)

### Familiar Command Forms

The command forms for *tu* and *voi* are identical with the present tense forms, except that in verbs of the first conjugation the *-i* ending of the *tu* form changes to *-a*.

| | |
|---|---|
| *parlare* (to speak) | parla! (fam. sing.)—speak! |
| | parlate! (fam. pl., also sing.)—speak! |
| *vedere* (to see) | vedi! (fam. sing.)—see! |
| | vedete! (fam. pl., also sing.)—see! |
| *partire* (to depart) | parti! (fam. sing.)—depart! |
| | partite! (fam. pl., also sing.)—depart! |
| *finire* (to finish) | finisci! (fam. sing.)—finish! |
| | finite! (fam. pl., also sing.)—finish! |

For irregular verbs only the following forms must be learned, since they are different from the present tense:

| | |
|---|---|
| *fare* (to do) | fa' (fam. sing.)—do! |
| *dare* (to give) | da' (fam. sing.)—give! |
| *stare* (to be) | sta' (fam. sing.)—be! |
| *andare* (to go) | va' (fam. sing.)—go! |
| *dire* (to say) | di' (fam. sing.)—say! |

## Review Table of Command Forms

| | FIRST CONJUGATION | SECOND CONJUGATION | THIRD CONJUGATION |
|---|---|---|---|
| (fam. sing.) | parla | vendi | parti |
| (polite sing.) | parli | venda | parta |
| (first person pl.) | parliamo | vendiamo | partiamo |
| (fam. pl., also sing.) | parlate | vendete | partite |
| (polite pl.) | parlino | vendano | partano |

## The Present Perfect Tense

In Italian, as in English, there are several ways of expressing what happened in the past. The most useful of the past tenses in Italian is the present perfect, which, as far as meaning is concerned, corresponds most closely to the simple English past: "I went", "I left", "I bought", although it is, in form, more closely related to the English present perfect: "I have gone", "I have left", "I have bought". The present perfect tense consists of two parts: the present tense of the helping verb (*avere* (to have) or *essere* (to be)) and the past participle.

## The Past Participle

In Italian, the past participle is formed by dropping the infinitive ending -*are*, -*ere*, -*ire* and adding -*ato* to verbs of the first conjugation, -*uto* to verbs of the second conjugation and -*ito* to verbs of the third conjugation.

| | |
|---|---|
| and*are* (to go) | and*ato* (gone) |
| ved*ere* (to see) | ved*uto* (seen) |
| sent*ire* (to hear) | sent*ito* (heard) |

Many past participles, especially in the second conjugation, are irregular. Here are some of the most common:

| | |
|---|---|
| nascere (to be born) | nato (born) |
| scrivere (to write) | scritto (written) |
| leggere (to read) | letto (read) |
| fare (to do, to make) | fatto (done, made) |
| dire (to say) | detto (said) |
| morire (to die) | morto (dead) |
| rispondere (to answer) | risposto (answered) |
| venire (to come) | venuto (come) |
| conoscere (to know) | conosciuto (known) |
| scendere (to go down) | sceso (gone down) |
| chiudere (to close) | chiuso (closed) |
| rompere (to break) | rotto (broken) |

## The Helping Verbs *Avere* and *Essere*

The Italian present perfect, an otherwise "easy" tense, presents one difficulty: the speaker must know whether the helping verb to be used in a particular case is *essere* (to be) or *avere* (to have). The general rule is that verbs of motion which do not take a direct object ("I *went* to the dentist") are conjugated with *essere*, while other verbs are conjugated with *avere*.

Since it may be difficult for you to determine which are the verbs of motion that do not take a direct object, simply remember a few of the most common verbs used with *essere*. Here is a list:

| | |
|---|---|
| entrare (to enter) | uscire (to go out) |
| partire (to depart) | andare (to go) |
| nascere (to be born) | morire (to die) |
| venire (to come) | scendere (to go down) |

The past participle of a verb conjugated with *essere* actually becomes a kind of adjective. It is therefore natural that it must agree with the subject.

| | |
|---|---|
| Maria è andat*a*. | Mary has gone. |
| Giovanni è andat*o*. | John has gone. |

## The Present Perfect of the Model Verbs

FIRST CONJUGATION

| | |
|---|---|
| ho parlato | I spoke, I have spoken |
| hai parlato | you (fam. sing.) spoke, have spoken |
| ha parlato | he (she, it) spoke, has spoken; you (polite sing.) spoke, have spoken |
| abbiamo parlato | we spoke, have spoken |

| avete parlato | you (fam. pl., also sing.) spoke, have spoken |
| hanno parlato | they spoke, have spoken; you (polite pl.) spoke, have spoken |

## SECOND CONJUGATION

| ho scritto* | I wrote, have written |
| hai scritto | you (fam. sing.) wrote, have written |
| ha scritto | he (she, it) wrote, has written; you (polite sing.) wrote, have written |
| abbiamo scritto | we wrote, have written |
| avete scritto | you (fam. pl., also sing.) wrote, have written |
| hanno scritto | they wrote, have written; you (polite pl.) wrote, have written |

## THIRD CONJUGATION

| sono† partito (-a) | I departed, have departed |
| sei partito (-a) | you (fam. sing.) departed, have departed |
| è partito (-a) | he (she, it) departed, has departed; you (polite sing.) departed, have departed |
| siamo partiti (-e) | we departed, have departed |
| siete partiti (-e) | you (fam. pl., also sing.) departed, |
| siete partito (-a) | have departed |
| sono partiti (-e) | they departed, have departed; you (polite pl.) departed, have departed |

* *Scrivere* has an irregular past participle. We are using *scrivere* as a model verb for the sake of variety.

† *Partire* is one of the verbs conjugated with *essere*.

## The Past Definite Tense

Though the present perfect tense is probably the most useful of the past tenses for the beginner, it is also important for you to be acquainted with the past definite or preterite. This tense is often used interchangeably with the present perfect, especially in some parts of Italy. It is more difficult than the present perfect because you have to learn a set of new endings and also because a large number of verbs are irregular in this tense.

### The Past Definite of the Model Verbs

FIRST CONJUGATION

| | |
|---|---|
| parlai | I spoke |
| parlasti | you (fam, sing.) spoke |
| parlò | he (she, it) spoke; you (polite sing.) spoke |
| parlammo | we spoke |
| parlaste | you (fam. pl., also sing.) spoke |
| parlarono | they spoke; you (polite pl.) spoke |

SECOND CONJUGATION

| | |
|---|---|
| vendei | I sold |
| vendesti | you (fam. sing.) sold |
| vendè | he (she, it) sold; you (polite sing.) sold |
| vendemmo | we sold |
| vendeste | you (fam. pl., also sing.) sold |
| venderono | they sold; you (polite pl.) sold |

THIRD CONJUGATION

| | |
|---|---|
| partii | I departed (*or* went away, left) |
| partisti | you (fam. sing.) departed |
| partì | he (she, it) departed; you (polite sing.) departed |

| partimmo | we departed |
| partiste | you (fam. pl., also sing.) departed |
| partirono | they departed; you (polite pl.) departed |

Observations on the Past Definite of the Model Verbs:

You have probably noticed that the characteristic conjugation vowel (*a* for verbs ending in *-are*; *e* for verbs ending in *-ere*; *i* for verbs ending in *-ire*) appears in every form of the past definite, except in the third person singular of the first conjugation verbs (parl*ò*). Apart from the conjugation vowel, the endings in the three conjugations are identical (parl*aste*, vend*este*, part*iste*).

## The Past Definite of Irregular Verbs

We have said that many Italian verbs are irregular in the past definite tense. However, there is a definite pattern in their irregularity: (1) three forms of the irregular past definites are always regular (second person singular, first person plural, second person plural); (2) the three irregular forms (first person singular, third person singular, third person plural) always have the same irregular root. Here is the Past Definite of *rispondere* (to answer):

| *risposi | I answered |
| rispondesti | you (fam. sing.) answered |
| *rispose | he (she, it) answered; you (polite sing.) answered |
| rispondemmo | we answered |
| rispondeste | you (fam. pl., also sing.) answered |
| *risposero | they answered; you (polite pl.) answered |

* The original infinitives of *fare* and *dire* (*facere* and *dicere*) are used in the past definite tense. We therefore have: *facesti, facemmo, faceste; dicesti, dicemmo, diceste.* Some less commonly used verbs follow a similar pattern.

The starred forms are irregular, but since they always follow the same pattern, you need memorize only the first person singular (*risposi*) and change the -*i* to -*e* and -*ero* to get the other two irregular persons (the third person singular and the third person plural).

## Common Irregular Past Definites

| | |
|---|---|
| avere (to have) | ebbi (I had) |
| nascere (to be born) | nacqui (I was born) |
| scrivere (to write) | scrissi (I wrote) |
| leggere (to read) | lessi (I read) |
| rispondere (to answer) | risposi (I answered) |
| venire (to come) | venni (I came) |
| conoscere (to know) | conobbi (I knew) |
| scendere (to go down) | scesi (I went down) |
| chiudere (to close) | chiusi (I closed) |
| chiedere (to ask) | chiesi (I asked) |
| *fare (to do, to make) | feci (I did) |
| *dire (to say) | dissi (I said) |

## The Past Definite of *essere* and *dare*

These two verbs contain irregularities which are not covered in the preceding section and must therefore be memorized in their entirety.

### *Essere*

| | |
|---|---|
| fui | I was |
| fosti | you (fam. sing.) were |
| fu | he (she, it) was; you (polite sing.) were |
| fummo | we were |
| foste | you (fam. pl., also sing.) were |
| furono | they were; you (polite pl.) were |

## Dare

| | |
|---|---|
| diedi | I gave |
| desti | you (fam. sing.) gave |
| diede | he (she, it) gave; you (polite sing.) gave |
| demmo | we gave |
| deste | you (fam. pl., also sing.) gave |
| diedero | they gave; you (polite pl.) gave |

## The Imperfect Tense

The imperfect tense is used to tell what was happening or what used to happen in the past. It is also the tense of description in the past. It is extremely simple to conjugate a verb in the imperfect tense, since all verbs with the exception of *essere* form their imperfect in the same way. The endings of the three conjugations are identical, but each conjugation keeps its characteristic vowel.

## The Imperfect Tense of the Model Verbs

### FIRST CONJUGATION

| | |
|---|---|
| parlavo | I spoke, used to speak, was speaking |
| parlavi | you (fam. sing.) spoke, used to speak, were speaking |
| parlava | he (she, it) spoke, used to speak, was speaking; you (polite sing.) spoke, used to speak, were speaking |
| parlavamo | we spoke, used to speak, were speaking |
| parlavate | you (fam. pl., also sing.) spoke, used to speak, were speaking |
| parlavano | they spoke, used to speak, were speaking; you (polite pl.) spoke, used to speak, were speaking |

### SECOND CONJUGATION

| | |
|---|---|
| vendevo | I sold, used to sell, was selling |
| vendevi | you (fam. sing.) sold, used to sell, were selling |
| vendeva | he (she, it) sold, used to sell, was selling; you (polite sing.) sold, used to sell, were selling |
| vendevamo | we sold, used to sell, were selling |
| vendevate | you (fam. pl., also sing.) sold, used to sell, were selling |
| vendevano | they sold, used to sell, were selling; you (polite pl.) sold, used to sell, were selling |

### THIRD CONJUGATION

| | |
|---|---|
| partivo | I departed, used to depart, was departing |
| partivi | you (fam. sing.) departed, used to depart, were departing |
| partiva | he (she, it) departed, used to depart, was departing; you (polite sing.) departed, used to depart, were departing |
| partivamo | we departed, used to depart, were departing |
| partivate | you (fam. pl., also sing.) departed, used to depart, were departing |
| partivano | they departed, used to depart, were departing; you (polite pl.) departed, used to depart, were departing |

## The Imperfect Tense of *essere*

| | |
|---|---|
| ero | I was, used to be |
| eri | you (fam. sing.) were, used to be |
| era | he (she, it) was, used to be; you (polite sing.) were, used to be |

| eravamo | we were, used to be |
| eravate | you (fam. pl., also sing.) were, used to be |
| erano | they were, used to be; you (polite pl.) were, used to be |

## The Uses of the Imperfect Tense

The following sentences illustrate the differences in use between the imperfect and the present perfect and the past definite tenses. Generally speaking, the *imperfect* is the tense used to describe something in the past, or to refer to something which used to happen or was happening in the past. The *present perfect* and the *past definite* both refer to a single completed action which happened at some definite time in the past.

Lo *vedevo* ogni giorno.
(Him I used to see every day.)
I *used to see* him every day.

Lo *vidi* ieri.
(Him I saw yesterday.)
I *saw* him yesterday.

L'*ho visto* stamani.
(Him I have seen this morning.)
I *saw* him this morning.

*Leggevo* quando *suonò* il campanello.
I *was reading* when he *rang* the bell.

Dove *andavi* quando ti *ho visto*?
(Where you were going when you I have seen?)
Where *were* you *going* when I *saw* you?

Quando *eravamo* bambini *giocavamo* tutto il giorno.
When we *were* children, we *used to play* all day.

Verbs which by their very nature express an attitude or a condition, a state of being or a state of mind, rather than an action, are those most frequently used in the imperfect. Here are some of the important ones:

volere (to want)      sperare (to hope)
credere (to think, believe)      sapere (to know)
potere (to be able)      essere (to be)

Non *sapevo* se sarebbero venuti.
(Not I knew if they would have come.)
I *did*n't *know* whether they would come.

*Eravamo* in quattro.
(We were in four.)
There *were* four of us.

*Volevo* vederla.      I *wanted* to see her.
Non *avevamo* denaro.      We *had* no money.

## The Pluperfect Tense

The pluperfect is a compound tense, like the present perfect. But instead of being formed with the present tense of the helping verb and the past participle, it is formed with the *imperfect tense* of the helping verb and the past participle. It is used, as in English, to refer to an action which *had* taken place prior to another action in the past. The helping verb is either *avere* or *essere*, according to the rule discussed on page 74.

## The Pluperfect Tense of the Model Verbs

### FIRST CONJUGATION

| | |
|---|---|
| avevo parlato | I had spoken |
| avevi parlato | you (fam. sing.) had spoken |
| aveva parlato | he (she, it) had spoken; you (polite sing.) had spoken |
| avevamo parlato | we had spoken |
| avevate parlato | you (fam. pl., also sing.) had spoken |
| avevano parlato | they had spoken; you (polite pl.) had spoken |

### SECOND CONJUGATION

| | |
|---|---|
| avevo venduto | I had sold |
| avevi venduto | you (fam. sing.) had sold |
| aveva venduto | he (she, it) had sold; you (polite sing.) had sold |
| avevamo venduto | we had sold |
| avevate venduto | you (fam. pl., also sing.) had sold |
| avevano venduto | they had sold; you (polite pl.) had sold |

### THIRD CONJUGATION

| | |
|---|---|
| ero partito (-a) | I had departed |
| eri partito (-a) | you (fam. sing.) had departed |
| era partito (-a) | he (she, it) had departed; you (polite sing.) had departed |
| eravamo partiti (-e) | we had departed |
| eravate partiti (-e) | you (fam. pl., also sing.) had departed |
| eravate partito (-a) | |
| erano partiti (-e) | they had departed; you (polite pl.) had departed |

## Use of the Pluperfect Tense

> Non *ero* mai *stato* in Italia.
> I *had* never *been* in Italy.
> Gli *avevo scritto* prima di partire.
> I *had written* him before leaving.

For the sake of completeness, we must mention that there is a *second pluperfect tense* in Italian, formed with the past definite tense of the helping verb and the past participle: *ebbi visto* (I had seen), *avesti visto* (you had seen), etc. This tense is used in a dependent clause. But as a beginning student you should avoid long, complicated sentences. You will therefore have little use for this second tense.

## The Future Tense

The future tense (in English, *will* or *shall* plus the infinitive: "I shall go") is formed by dropping the final -*e* of the infinitive and adding the endings -*ò*, -*ai*, -*à*, -*emo*, -*ete*, -*anno*. In verbs of the first conjugation the *a* of the infinitive changes to *e* (cant*are* (to sing), cant*erò* (I shall sing)).

## The Future Tense of the Model Verbs

FIRST CONJUGATION

| | |
|---|---|
| parlerò | I shall speak |
| parlerai | you (fam. sing.) will speak |
| parlerà | he (she, it) will speak; you (polite sing.) will speak |
| parleremo | we shall speak |
| parlerete | you (fam. pl., also sing.) will speak |
| parleranno | they will speak; you (polite pl.) will speak |

## SECOND CONJUGATION

| | |
|---|---|
| venderò | I shall sell |
| venderai | you (fam. sing.) will sell |
| venderà | he (she, it) will sell; you (polite sing.) will sell |
| venderemo | we shall sell |
| venderete | you (fam. pl., also sing.) will sell |
| venderanno | they will sell; you (polite pl.) will sell |

### THIRD CONJUGATION

| | |
|---|---|
| partirò | I shall leave |
| partirai | you (fam. sing.) will leave |
| partirà | he (she, it) will leave; you (polite sing.) will leave |
| partiremo | we shall leave |
| partirete | you (fam. pl., also sing.) will leave |
| partiranno | they will leave; you (polite pl.) will leave |

## The Future Tense of Irregular Verbs

### VERBS IN WHICH THE CONJUGATION VOWEL IS DROPPED

A number of common verbs are irregular in the future because the conjugation vowel (and*a*re, av*e*re) is dropped before the future endings are added.

| | |
|---|---|
| andare (to go) | andrò, andrai, andrà, andremo, andrete, andranno |
| avere (to have) | avrò, avrai, avrà, avremo, avrete, avranno |
| potere (to be able) | potrò, potrai, potrà, potremo, potrete, potranno |
| sapere (to know) | saprò, saprai, saprà, sapremo, saprete, sapranno |

dovere (to have to)  dovrò, dovrai, dovrà, dovremo, dovrete, dovranno

vivere (to live)  vivrò, vivrai, vivrà, vivremo, vivrete, vivranno

vedere (to see)  vedrò, vedrai, vedrà, vedremo, vedrete, vedranno

## VERBS IN WHICH THE CONJUGATION VOWEL IS DROPPED AND THE PRECEDING CONSONANT BECOMES "R"

In a number of common verbs the dropping of the conjugation vowel brings with it an additional change before the future endings are added.

tenere (to hold)  terrò, terrai, terrà, terremo, terrete, terranno

rimanere (to remain)  rimarrò, rimarrai, rimarrà, rimarremo, rimarrete, rimarranno

volere (to want)  vorrò, vorrai, vorrà, vorremo, vorrete, vorranno

venire (to come)  verrò, verrai, verrà, verremo, verrete, verranno

### THE FUTURE TENSE OF "ESSERE"

| | |
|---|---|
| sarò | I shall be |
| sarai | you (fam. sing.) will be |
| sarà | he (she, it) will be; you (polite sing.) will be |
| saremo | we shall be |
| sarete | you (fam. pl., also sing.) will be |
| saranno | they will be; you (polite pl.) will be |

## The Uses of the Future Tense

Study the following sentences which illustrate the use of the future in Italian. In general, English and Italian use corresponds.

Che cosa *farà* domani sera?
What *will* you *do* tomorrow evening?

Credo che *andremo* a visitare degli amici.
I think that we *shall go* to visit some friends.

*Ritorneremo* presto però.
We *shall return* early, however.

Quando *partirete*?
When *will* you *leave*?

There is one use of the future in Italian which has no equivalent in English. The future is used in Italian to express what is probable in the present.

*Saranno* le tre.
(They will be the three.)
It *is probably* three o'clock.

*Sarà* il presidente che parla.
It *is probably* the president who is speaking.

In Italian there is also a *future perfect tense*, formed with the future tense of the helping verb and the past participle. This tense is used to refer to an action that will have taken place before another action in the future. In English the present perfect is frequently used instead of the future perfect tense.

Quando *avrò scritto* la lettera, l'imposterò.
(When I *shall have written* the letter, I shall post it.)
When I *have written* the letter, I shall post it.

## The Conditional Mood

The conditional (in English, *would* plus the infinitive) is formed by taking the stem used in the future and adding the endings *-ei, -esti, -ebbe, -emmo, -este, -ebbero*. Whatever irregularities appear in the future will therefore also appear in the conditional.

## The Conditional of the Model Verb *Parlare*

| | |
|---|---|
| parlerei | I would speak |
| parleresti | you (fam. sing.) would speak |
| parlerebbe | he (she, it) would speak; you (polite sing.) would speak |
| parleremmo | we would speak |
| parlereste | you (fam. pl., also sing.) would speak |
| parlerebbero | they would speak; you (polite pl.) would speak |

## The Conditional of Irregular Verbs

| | |
|---|---|
| andare (to go) | andrei, andresti, andrebbe, andremmo, andreste, andrebbero |
| essere (to be) | sarei, saresti, sarebbe, saremmo, sareste, sarebbero |
| avere (to have) | avrei, avresti, avrebbe, avremmo, avreste, avrebbero |
| sapere (to know) | saprei, sapresti, saprebbe, sapremmo, sapreste, saprebbero |
| volere (to want) | vorrei, vorresti, vorrebbe, vorremmo, vorreste, vorrebbero |

## The Uses of the Conditional

The conditional is used in Italian as it is in English (I *would come*, if I could). It is also used, contrary to English, to express what is reported by hearsay.

> Io non lo *farei*.
> I *would* not *do* it.
>
> Mi *farebbe* il piacere di aprire la porta?
> *Would* you *do* me the favour of opening the door?
>
> Secondo lui, *sarebbe* tempo di andare.
> According to him, it *is* time to go.

There is also a *conditional perfect*, formed with the conditional of the helping verb and the past participle. It is used like the corresponding tense in English and also to express what was reported by hearsay.

> L'*avrei fatto* con piacere.
> I *would have done* it with pleasure.
>
> Secondo lui, *sarebbe stato* tempo di andare.
> According to him, it *was* time to go.

A further discussion of the conditional in if-sentences will be found on pages 94 and 95.

### The Subjunctive Mood

The subjunctive, which survives in English in sentences such as "If I *were* to tell you, you wouldn't believe me", occurs much more frequently in Italian. It is therefore important that you know something about it and that you be familiar with its forms.

With very few exceptions, the subjunctive occurs only in dependent clauses. Although it is usually possible to break up a long, complex sentence into two or more short, simple sentences, there are cases where this is impossible. Instead of saying, "Here is the girl whom we met yesterday", we can very well say, "Here is the girl. We met her yesterday." But how else can we express ideas such as, "I want you to open the window" or "I would come if I could", except in the way just stated? We shall limit our explanation of the uses of the subjunctive to these two situations and just a few others.

## Tenses of the Subjunctive

### THE PRESENT SUBJUNCTIVE OF THE MODEL VERB "PARLARE"

| | |
|---|---|
| che io parli | that I speak |
| che tu parli | that you (fam. sing.) speak |
| che egli (Lei) parli | that he (you) speak |
| che noi parliamo | that we speak |
| che voi parliate | that you (fam. pl., also sing.) speak |
| che essi (Loro) parlino | that they (you) speak |

### THE PRESENT PERFECT SUBJUNCTIVE OF THE MODEL VERB "PARLARE"

| | |
|---|---|
| che io abbia parlato | that I have spoken |
| che tu abbia parlato | that you (fam. sing.) have spoken |
| che egli (Lei) abbia parlato | that he (you) have spoken |
| che noi abbiamo parlato | that we have spoken |
| che voi abbiate parlato | that you (fam. pl., also sing.) have spoken |
| che essi (Loro) abbiano parlato | that they (you) have spoken |

### THE PAST SUBJUNCTIVE OF THE MODEL VERB "PARLARE"

| | |
|---|---|
| che io parlassi | that I spoke |
| che tu parlassi | that you (fam. sing.) spoke |
| che egli (Lei) parlasse | that he (you) spoke |
| che noi parlassimo | that we spoke |
| che voi parlaste | that you (fam. pl., also sing.) spoke |
| che essi (Loro) parlassero | that they (you) spoke |

### THE PAST PERFECT SUBJUNCTIVE OF THE MODEL VERB "PARLARE"

| | |
|---|---|
| che io avessi parlato | that I had spoken |
| che tu avessi parlato | that you (fam. sing.) had spoken |
| che egli (Lei) avesse parlato | that he (you) had spoken |
| che noi avessimo parlato | that we had spoken |
| che voi aveste parlato | that you (fam. pl., also sing.) had spoken |
| che essi (Loro) avessero parlato | that they (you) had spoken |

The Present and Past Subjunctive of the Model Verbs *vendere* and *partire*:

### THE PRESENT SUBJUNCTIVE

| | |
|---|---|
| che io venda | che io parta |
| che tu venda | che tu parta |
| che egli (Lei) venda | che egli (Lei) parta |
| che noi vendiamo | che noi partiamo |
| che voi vendiate | che voi partiate |
| che essi (Loro) vendano | che essi (Loro) partano |

### THE PAST SUBJUNCTIVE

| | |
|---|---|
| che io vendessi | che io partissi |
| che tu vendessi | che tu partissi |
| che egli (Lei) vendesse | che egli (Lei) partisse |
| che noi vendessimo | che noi partissimo |
| che voi vendeste | che voi partiste |
| che essi (Loro) vendessero | che essi (Loro) partissero |

Observations on the Subjunctive Forms of Regular Verbs:

**1.** In the present subjunctive the first, second and third persons singular are identical in each conjugation.

**2.** The first person plural of the present subjunctive is the same as the first person plural of the present indicative.

**3.** In the second and third conjugations the endings are identical.

**4.** Whatever vowel appears in the ending of the singular forms of the present subjunctive is also used in the third person plural (cant*i*, cant*i*no; vend*a*, vend*a*no).

**5.** In the past subjunctive the endings are identical for the three conjugations, except that each conjugation keeps its conjugation vowel (parl*a*ssi, vend*e*ssi, part*i*ssi).

**6.** The past subjunctive of all verbs, just like the imperfect, is regular. The only exception is *essere* (fossi, fossi, fosse, fossimo, foste, fossero).

**7.** The present perfect subjunctive and the past perfect subjunctive are formed respectively with the present subjunctive and the past subjunctive of the helping verb plus the past participle.

## The Present Subjunctive of Irregular Verbs

Many verbs which are irregular in the present indicative are also irregular in the present subjunctive. Here is a list of the most common:

| INFINITIVE | PRESENT INDICATIVE | PRESENT SUBJUNCTIVE |
|---|---|---|
| fare | faccio | faccia, facciamo, facciate, facciano |
| andare | vado | vada, andiamo, andiate, vadano |
| volere | voglio | voglia, vogliamo, vogliate, vogliano |
| venire | vengo | venga, veniamo, veniate, vengano |
| bere | bevo | beva, beviamo, beviate, bevano |
| potere | posso | possa, possiamo, possiate, possano |
| avere | ho | abbia, abbiamo, abbiate, abbiano |
| essere | sono | sia, siamo, siate, siano |

This is an excellent opportunity to review irregular verbs. Turn back to page 68 and go through the whole list, reciting the present indicative and the present subjunctive for each verb.

## The Uses of the Subjunctive

The subjunctive is commonly used in the following situations:

**1.** After a verb of desiring in the main clause of a sentence, the subjunctive is used in the dependent clause when the dependent clause has a different subject.

Voglio che tu *apra* la porta.

(I want that you *open* the door.)

I want you to open the door.

(Compare: *Voglio aprire la porta*, I want to open the door [that is, myself].)

**2.** After verbs of doubt:

> Non so se egli *venga*.
> I don't know if he *is coming*.

**3.** After many impersonal verbs:

> È necessario che loro *partano*.
> It is necessary that they leave.

> Mi sembra che tu *abbia* ragione.
> It seems to me that you *are* right.

> Mi piace che Lei *sia venuto*.
> I am pleased that you *have come*.

**4.** To express a wish:

> *Viva* la libertà!
> (Long) *live* freedom!

**5.** In "contrary-to-fact" if-sentences:
(referring to the present:)

> Se *fossi* più giovane, la sposerei.
> If I *were* younger [but I'm not], I'd marry her.

(referring to the past:)

> Se *fossi stato* più giovane, l'avrei sposata.
> If I *had been younger* [but I wasn't], I'd have married
> her.

NOTE: In these "contrary-to-fact" if-sentences, in which the if's cannot be fulfilled, the past subjunctive is normally used in the if-clause and the conditional in the main clause, when the present is referred to (if I were younger *now*). When referring to the past (what might have been), use the past perfect subjunctive in the if-clause and the conditional perfect in the main clause. (A simple if-sentence, with possibility of fulfilment, does not require the subjunctive: *Se posso, verrò*, If I can, I'll come.)

## Reflexive Verbs

### Comparison of Reflexive Verbs in English and Italian

In English we say: "I get up", "I wash", "I shave", "I dress". In each case the action of the verb refers back to the subject. We might also say: "I wash myself", "I shave myself", "I dress myself". This is what is done in Italian where the reflexive pronoun (*mi, ti, si, ci, vi, si*) must be used with all reflexive verbs. In Italian the reflexive pronoun precedes the verb, except in those cases where, like the object pronoun, it follows the verb and is written as one word with it (see page 51).

### The Present Tense of Reflexive Verbs

*guardarsi* (to look at oneself): Note that the reflexive pronoun *si* is added to the infinitive after the final *e* has been dropped.

| | |
|---|---|
| *mi* guardo | I look at myself |
| *ti* guardi | you (fam. sing.) look at yourself |
| *si* guarda | he (she, it) looks at himself (herself, itself); you (polite sing.) look at yourself |
| *ci* guardiamo | we look at ourselves |
| *vi* guardate | you (fam. pl., also sing.) look at yourself (yourselves) |
| *si* guardano | they look at themselves; you (polite pl.) look at yourselves |

## The Present Perfect Tense of Reflexive Verbs

Note that reflexive verbs are all conjugated with *essere* and that the past participle agrees with the subject.

| | |
|---|---|
| *mi* sono guardato (-a) | I looked at myself |
| *ti* sei guardato (-a) | you (fam. sing.) looked at yourself |
| *si* è guardato (-a) | he (she, it) looked at himself (herself); you (polite sing.) looked at yourself |
| *ci* siamo guardati (-e) | we looked at ourselves |
| *vi* siete guardati (-e) | you (fam. pl., also sing.) looked at |
| *vi* siete guardato (-a) | yourself (yourselves) |
| *si* sono guardati (-e) | they looked at themselves; you (polite pl.) looked at yourselves |

## The Command Form or Imperative of Reflexive Verbs

| | |
|---|---|
| guarda*ti* | look (fam. sing.) at yourself |
| *si* guardi | look (polite sing.) at yourself |
| guardiamo*ci* | let us look at one another, at ourselves |
| guardate*vi* | look (fam. pl., also sing.) at yourself (yourselves) |
| *si* guardino | look (polite pl.) at yourselves |

## Important Reflexive Verbs

Reflexive verbs are more frequent in Italian than in English. *Alzarsi* (to get up), *sedersi* (to sit down), *vestirsi* (to get dressed), for instance, are reflexive in Italian while they are not in English.

| | |
|---|---|
| divertirsi | to have a good time |
| coricarsi | to lie down |

| svegliarsi | to wake up |
| sentirsi bene (or male) | to feel well (or ill) |
| sposarsi | to get married |
| farsi la barba | to shave |
| togliersi | to take off (as clothing) |
| avvicinarsi | to come closer |
| riposarsi | to rest |

## Uses of the Reflexive

The following sentences illustrate reflexive and non-reflexive uses of verbs. Study them carefully.

Mia zia è vecchia. Non *sente* bene.
My aunt is old. She doesn't *hear* well.

Ho un raffreddore. Non *mi sento* bene.
I have a cold. I don't *feel* well.

*Scrivo* spesso ai miei amici.
I often *write* my friends.

*Ci scriviamo* spesso.
We often *write to one another*.

*Ho svegliato* mio fratello.
I *woke up* my brother.

*Si è svegliato* tardi stamani.
He *woke up* late this morning.

*Chiama* la guardia.
*Call* the police officer.

*Mi chiamo* Carlo.
(Myself I call Charles.)
*I am called* Charles.

The reflexive is often used to avoid use of the possessive

adjective with parts of the body or with articles of clothing. Observe the following examples:

*Mi metto* le scarpe.    I am putting on my shoes.
*Mi lavo* le mani.    I wash my hands.

In Italian the reflexive is also used where English uses an impersonal construction such as "Here one speaks English", or "They say it is so", or "We do it that way", or where in English the passive would be used: "This is how it is said."

Qui *si parla* inglese.    Here one speaks English.
Come *si dice* "pencil" in italiano?
How do you say "pencil" in Italian?

*Si va* al cinema?
Are we going to the movies?

*Si fa* così.
It is done this way.

*Si fanno* molte cose.
Many things are done.

*Si deve* comprare il biglietto prima d'entrare.
You must buy the ticket before entering.

### The Passive Voice

In Italian the passive is formed as it is in English, by using the verb "to be" (*essere*) with the past participle: "The book *was written* by Mr. Jones." The reflexive construction, discussed above, is often used instead of the passive in Italian. However, when the person doing the action is mentioned it is impossible to use the reflexive, and the passive must be used. The following examples will make this point clear:

Questa lettera *fu scritta* \* dalla segretaria.
This letter *was written* by the secretary.

*Si scrivono* molte lettere in un anno.
Many letters *are written* in a year.

Questo palazzo *fu costruito* da un architetto famoso.
This building *was built* by a famous architect.

*Si sono costruiti* molti palazzi nuovi.
Many new buildings *have been built*.

## Prepositions and Infinitives

### Verbs Followed Directly by the Infinitive

As in English ("I must go home"), many common Italian verbs are followed directly by the infinitive without an intervening preposition. Study these examples:

*Vuole* andare al cinema?
Do you want to go to the cinema?

*Devo* partire domani mattina.
I must leave tomorrow morning.

*Dobbiamo* uscire presto.
We must go out early.

*Faccia* chiudere la finestra.
Have the window closed.

Mi *potrebbe* prestare del denaro?
Could you lend me some money?

Le *piace* ballare?
Do you like to dance?

---

\* Note that the past participle agrees with the subject, as it always does when the verb is conjugated with *essere*.

As is apparent from the last example, there are many cases where in English you will find the infinitive preceded by "to" while no preposition is used in Italian.

### Verbs Followed by *a* or *di* before the Infinitive

Study the following sentences:

Impariamo *a* leggere e scrivere.
We are learning to read and write.

M'insegna *a* nuotare.
He is teaching me to swim.

Cominciamo *a* capire meglio.
**We are beginning to understand better.**

Mi aiuti *a* chiudere la finestra.
Help me to close the window.

Ho deciso *di* partire.
I decided to leave.

Gli ho domandato *di* portarmelo.
I asked him to bring it to me.

Le dico *di* non disturbarmi.
I tell you not to bother me.

Ha dimenticato *di* farlo.
He forgot to do it.

Only repeated use will help you to remember which verbs are followed by *di*, which by *a* and which take no preposition at all. For the beginner it is sufficient to remember the examples given.

## The Present Participle and the Infinitive

In English the present participle is used after prepositions (before *leaving*, after *eating*, without *thinking*). In Italian it is never so used, but the infinitive is used instead.

| | |
|---|---|
| prima di *partire* | before leaving |
| senza *parlare* | without speaking |
| all'*entrare* | upon entering |
| *dopo *essere arrivati* | after arriving (after having arrived) |

*Prima di partire* dobbiamo pagare il conto.
*Before leaving* we must pay the bill.

Se ne andò *senza parlare*.
He left *without speaking*.

*All'entrare* dell'attrice, il pubblico si è alzato.
*Upon* the actress's *entering*, the audience rose.

*Dopo essere arrivati*, si misero a sedere.
*After arriving*, they sat down.

### Idiomatic Constructions

We have seen that there are many parallel constructions in English and Italian. But there are also many idiomatic expressions in Italian which have no exact parallel in English. These cannot be translated literally, nor can they always be explained grammatically or logically. It is important to learn most of these expressions because without them you would be unable to say many of the common things you are most anxious to say.

* Note that after *dopo* the compound infinitive (the infinitive of the helping verb and the past participle) must be used.

## The Verb *Piacere*

The English verb "to like" is translated by the Italian verb *piacere* (to please). In English you say, "I like Rome", or "I like Rome and Florence", but in Italian you must turn the sentence around to read, "Rome is pleasing to me", or "Rome and Florence are pleasing to me". *Piacere* is therefore used most frequently in the third person, singular and plural, and what is the subject in English becomes an indirect object pronoun in Italian.

| | | |
|---|---|---|
| mi | | I like |
| ti | | you (fam. sing.) like |
| gli | piace (it is pleasing) | he likes |
| le | | she likes |
| Le | piacciono (they are pleasing) | you (polite sing.) like |
| ci | | we like |
| vi | | you (fam. pl.) like |
| piace (piacciono) loro | | they like |
| piace (piacciono) Loro | | you (polite pl.) like |

Study the following sentences:

Mi piace ballare.
[To me it is pleasing to dance.]
I like to dance.

Le piacciono questi fiori?
[To you are pleasing these flowers?]
Do you like these flowers?

Ci è piaciuto il film ieri sera.
[To us was pleasing the film yesterday evening.]
We liked the movie last night.

Gli piacciono molto.
[To him they are pleasing very much.]
He likes them very much.

Mi sono piaciuti i fiori.
[To me were pleasing the flowers.]
I liked the flowers.

Piace viaggiare a tua sorella?
[Is it pleasing to travel for your sister?]
Does your sister like to travel?

Observe that *piacere* is conjugated with *essere* and that the past participle therefore agrees with the subject (the object in English).

## The Verb *fare*

*Fare* (to do, to make) is used in a variety of idiomatic expressions, where English uses other verbs.

**1.** Expressions of weather:

Che tempo *fa*?
[What weather *makes* it?]
How is the weather?

*Fa* bel (cattivo) tempo.
[It *makes* good (bad) weather.]
The weather is fine (bad).

*Fa* freddo.
[It *makes* cold.]
It is cold.

*Fa* molto caldo.
[It *makes* very hot.]
It is very hot.

Note however:

| | |
|---|---|
| Piove. | It is raining. |
| Tira vento. | The wind is blowing. |

**2.** Professions:

>Che cosa *fa* Suo padre?
>What does your father *do*?

>Mio padre *fa* il medico.
>[He exercises the profession of doctor.]
>My father is a doctor.

>*Faccio* il musicista.
>I am a musician.

**3.** *Fare* used in place of English "have":

>*Faccia* aprire la porta.
>Have the door opened.

>Mi *son fatto* fare un vestito.
>I had a dress made for myself.

>Le *ho fatto* scrivere una lettera.
>I had her write a letter (or, I had a letter written to her).

Note that in Italian the *infinitive* and not the past participle is used in this construction.

**4.** Other idiomatic uses:

| | |
|---|---|
| *fare* una domanda | to ask a question |
| *fare* un viaggio | to take a trip |
| *fare* un bagno | to have a bath |
| *fare* una passeggiata | to take a walk |
| *fare* colazione | to have breakfast or lunch |
| *fare* da mangiare | to prepare lunch or dinner |
| *fare* attenzione | to pay attention |
| *fare* un piacere | to do a favour |

| | |
|---|---|
| *fare* una conferenza | to give a lecture |
| *farsi* male | to hurt oneself |
| *farsi* ricco | to become rich |
| *farsi* la barba | to shave |
| Si *fa* tardi. | It is getting late. |
| Non *fa* niente. | It's all right. |

## The Verb *Avere*

"To be hungry, thirsty, warm, etc.," are rendered in Italian by the verb *avere* with the noun: "to have hunger, thirst, etc."

| | |
|---|---|
| *Ho* fame. | I am hungry. |
| *Ho* sete. | I am thirsty. |
| *Ho* caldo. | I am warm. |
| *Ho* freddo. | I am cold. |
| *Ho* fretta. | I am in a hurry. |
| *Ho* paura. | I am afraid. |
| *Hai* ragione. | You (fam. sing.) are right. |
| *Ho* sonno. | I am sleepy. |

Observe also:

*Ho* venticinque anni.
I am twenty-five years old.

*Ha* i capelli biondi e gli occhi azzurri.
His hair is blond and his eyes are blue.

Che cos'*hai*?
What is the matter with you (fam. sing.)?

Non *ho* niente.
Nothing is the matter with me.

## The Verbs *essere* and *stare*

Although *essere* and *stare* both mean "to be", they are not interchangeable. In English "to be" expresses many different ideas: "Rome and Florence *are* in Italy" (i.e. are located); "Two and two *are* four" (i.e. equal four); "We are sick" (i.e. condition); "We *are* going home" (part of the progressive). In Italian *essere* is used as a helping verb; *stare* is used to form the progressive. *Stare* is the verb used to refer to health in phrases such as *Sto bene* (I'm well) and *Come sta?* (How are you?). Study the following examples, which illustrate the different uses of *essere* and *stare*:

| | |
|---|---|
| Roma e Firenze *sono* in Italia. | Rome and Florence are in Italy. |
| *Siamo* ammalati. | We are ill. |
| *Siamo* arrivati. | We arrived. |
| *Stiamo* andando a casa. | We are going home. |
| *Stiamo* a Milano. | We live in Milan. |
| *Stiamo* bene. | We are well. |
| Come *sta?* | How are you (polite sing.)? |
| *Stiamo* per andare a casa. | We are about to go home. |
| Le piace *stare* in piedi? | Do you like to stand up? |
| *Stai* zitto! | Be (polite sing.) quiet! |
| *Stai* a sentire! | Just listen (fam. sing.) to this! |

### *C'è* and *ci sono*

*C'è* means "there is"; *ci sono*, "there are"; *c'era*, "there was"; *c'erano*, "there were".

| | |
|---|---|
| *C'è* ancora molto da fare. | *There is* still much to do. |
| *Ci sono* quattro posti liberi. | *There are* four empty places. |

| | |
|---|---|
| *C'era* molto da vedere. | *There was* much to be seen. |
| *C'erano* molte cose da vedere. | *There were* many things to be seen. |

## *Aver bisogno* and *Bisognare*

Confusion between these two expressions arises because of their similarity. *Aver bisogno di* is used to express a lack of something and translated literally as "to have need of". The impersonal verb *bisognare*, instead, means "to be necessary" and is followed by the subjunctive. Study these sentences:

| | |
|---|---|
| *Ho bisogno di* un paio di scarpe. | *I need* a pair of shoes. |
| *Bisogna* ch'egli parta. | *It is necessary* that he go. |

## The Verb *Volere*

*Volere* (to wish, to want) has a variety of uses:

| | |
|---|---|
| *Voglio* partire subito. | *I want* to leave at once. |
| *Vuol* farmi questo favore? | *Will* you do me this favour? |
| *Vorrei* andarci anch'io. | I, too, *would like* to go there. |
| Cosa *vuol* dire questa parola? | What does this word mean? |
| Ci *vogliono* due ore per andare da Bologna a Firenze. | It *takes* two hours to go from Bologna to Florence. |
| Come *vuole*. | As you *wish*. |
| *Voglio* bene a mia madre. | I love my mother. |

## The Verbs *Dare* and *Andare*

Some idioms with *dare*:

| | |
|---|---|
| *dar* ragione, *dar* torto | to agree, to disagree |
| *dare* la mano a | to shake hands with |
| *dare* del tu, del voi, del Lei | to use *tu, voi, Lei* in direct address |

Some idioms with *andare*:

| | |
|---|---|
| *andare* in automobile, in treno | to go by car, by train |
| *andare* a cavallo | to ride |
| Come *va*? | How goes it? |
| *Va* bene. | Very well. |

## The Verbs *Sapere* and *Conoscere*

Although both *sapere* and *conoscere* are translated by "to know", they are not interchangeable. Essentially, *sapere* means "to know" in the sense of "to have knowledge"; *conoscere*, in the sense of "to be acquainted with". *Conoscere* may also be used in the sense of "to meet", "to make the acquaintance of".

| | |
|---|---|
| *Sa* che ora è? | Do you *know* what time it is? |
| *Conosco* quel signore. | I *know* that gentleman. |
| Vorrei *conoscer*lo. | I'd like to *meet* him. |
| Non *sa* suonare il pianoforte. | He doesn't *know how* to play the piano. |
| Piacere di *conoscer*La! | Pleased to *meet* you! |
| *So* dov'è la stazione. | I *know* where the station is. |
| *Conosco* quell'albergo. | I *know* that hotel. |

# Some Useful Expressions

Study these useful expressions which have not appeared in the main body of this book.

| | |
|---|---|
| Che ore sono? | What time is it? (LIT. What hours are?) |
| Che ora è? | What time is it? (LIT. What hour is?) |
| Sono le otto e mezza. | It is half-past eight. |
| È mezzogiorno. | It is midday. |
| Mi mancano i miei. | I miss my family. |
| Non importa. | It doesn't matter. |
| Non ci pensi. | Don't worry about it. |
| Mi dispiace. | I'm sorry. |
| Peccato! | Too bad! What a pity! |
| Va bene. | All right. |
| Lei è molto gentile. | You are very kind. |
| Si diverta! | Have a good time! |
| Buon appetito! | Enjoy your meal! |
| Davvero! | Really! You don't say so! |
| Non va. | It's no good. |
| Buon giorno. | Good morning. |
| Buona sera. | Good evening. |
| Buona notte. | Good night. |
| Arrivederci. | Goodbye |
| Arrivederci a domani. | Goodbye until tomorrow. |
| A domani. | See you tomorrow. |
| Dopo pranzo | In the afternoon. (After lunch.) |
| Dopodomani. | The day after tomorrow. |

| | |
|---|---|
| Ieri l'altro. | The day before yesterday. |
| Subito. | At once. |
| Fra poco. | In a little while. |
| Finalmente. | Finally. At last. |
| Di nuovo. | Again. |
| Invece. | Instead |
| Bene. | Well. Good. |
| Forse. | Perhaps. |
| Quindi. | Therefore. |
| Almeno. | At least. |
| S'intende. | Of course. |
| Certo. | Certainly. |
| Come no! | Naturally! |
| Tutti | Everybody. |
| Tutto. | Everything. |
| Con piacere. | Willingly. With pleasure. |
| Molte grazie. | Many thanks. |
| Prego. | You're welcome. |
| Scusi. | Excuse me. |
| Permesso. | With your permission. |

# A Glossary of Grammatical Terms

## E. F. BLEILER

This section is intended to refresh your memory of grammatical terms or to clear up difficulties you may have had in understanding them. Before you work through the grammar you should have a reasonably clear idea what the parts of speech and parts of a sentence are. This is not for reasons of pedantry, but simply because it is easier to talk about grammar if we agree upon terms. Grammatical terminology is as necessary to the study of grammar as the names of automobile parts are to garage men.

This list is not exhaustive, and the definitions do not pretend to be complete, or to settle points of interpretation that grammarians have been disputing for several hundred years. It is a working analysis rather than a scholarly investigation. The definitions given, however, represent most typical English usage, and should serve for basic use in this book.

## The Parts of Speech

English words can be divided into eight important groups: nouns, adjectives, articles, verbs, adverbs, pronouns, prepositions and conjunctions. The boundaries between one group of words and another are sometimes vague and ill-felt in English, but a good dictionary can help you make decisions in doubtful cases. Always bear in mind, however, that the way a word is used in a sentence may be just as

111

important as the nature of the word itself in deciding what part of speech the word is.

**Nouns.** *Nouns* are the *words* for *things* of all *sorts*, whether these *things* are real *objects* that you can see, or *ideas*, or *places*, or *qualities*, or *groups*, or more abstract *things*. *Examples* of *words* that are *nouns* are *cat, vase, door, shrub, wheat, university, mercy, intelligence, ocean, plumber, pleasure, society, army*. If you are in *doubt* whether a given *word* is a *noun*, try putting the *word* "my" or "this" or "large" (or some other *adjective*) in *front* of it. If it makes *sense* in the *sentence* the *chances* are that the *word* in *question* is a *noun*. [All the *words* in *italics* in this *paragraph* are *nouns*.]

**Adjectives.** Adjectives are the words which describe or give you *specific* information about the *various* nouns in a sentence. They tell you size, colour, weight, pleasantness and many *other* qualities. *Such* words as *big, expensive, terrible, insipid, hot, delightful, ruddy, informative* are all *clear* adjectives. If you are in *any* doubt whether a *certain* word is an adjective, add -er to it, or put the word "more" or "too" in front of it. If it makes *good* sense in the sentence, and does not end in -ly, the chances are that it is an adjective. (Pronoun-adjectives will be described under pronouns.) [The adjectives in the *above* sentences are in italics.]

**Articles.** There are only two kinds of articles in English, and they are easy to remember. The definite article is "the" and the indefinite article is "a" or "an".

**Verbs.** Verbs *are* the words that *tell* what action, or condition, or relationship *is going* on. Such words as *was, is,* *jumps, achieved, keeps, buys, sells, has finished, run, will have, may, should pay, indicates are* all verb forms. *Observe* that a verb *can be composed* of more than one word, as *will have* and *should pay*, above; these *are called* compound verbs. As a rough guide for verbs, *try adding* -ed to the word you *are wondering* about, or *taking* off an -ed that *is* already there. If it *makes* sense the chances *are* that it *is* a verb. (This *does* not always *work*, since the so-called strong or irregular verbs *make* forms by *changing* their middle vowels, like *spring, sprang, sprung*.) [Verbs in this paragraph *are* in italics.]

**Adverbs.** An adverb is a word that supplies additional information about a verb, an adjective or another adverb. It *usually* indicates time, or manner, or place, or degree. It tells you *how*, or *when*, or *where*, or to what degree things are happening. Such words as *now, then, there, not, anywhere, never, somehow, always, very* and most words ending in -ly are *normally* adverbs. [Italicized words are adverbs.]

**Pronouns.** Pronouns are related to nouns, and take their place. (Some grammars and dictionaries group pronouns and nouns together as substantives.) *They* mention persons or objects of any sort without actually giving their names.

There are several different kinds of pronouns. (1) Personal pronouns: by a grammatical convention *I, we, me, mine, us, ours* are called first person pronouns, since *they* refer to the speaker; *you* and *yours* are called second person pronouns, since *they* refer to the person addressed; and *he, him, his, she, hers, they, them, theirs* are called third person pronouns, since *they* refer to the things or persons discussed. (2) Demonstrative pronouns: *this, that, these, those*. (3) Interrogative, or question, pronouns: *who, whom, what, whose, which.* (4) Relative pronouns, or pronouns *which* refer back to something already mentioned: *who, whom, that, which.* (5) Others: *some, any, anyone, no one, other, whichever, none,* etc.

Pronouns are difficult for *us,* since our categories are not as clear as in some other languages, and *we* use the same words for *what* foreign-language speakers see as different situations. First, our interrogative and relative pronouns overlap, and must be separated in translation. The easiest way is to observe whether a question is involved in the sentence. Examples: "*Which* [int.] do *you* like?" "The inn, *which* [rel.] was not far from Verona, had a restaurant." "*Who* [int.] is there?" "*I* don't know *who* [int.] was there." "The porter *who* [rel.] took our bags was Number 2132." *This* may seem to be a trivial difference to an English speaker, but in some languages *it* is very important.

Secondly, there is an overlap between pronouns and adjectives. In some cases the word "this", for example, is a pronoun; in other cases *it* is an adjective. *This* also holds true for *his, its, her, any, none, other, some, that, these, those* and many other words. Note whether the word in question stands alone or is associated with another word. Examples: "*This* [pronoun] is *mine.*" "This [adj.] taxi has no springs." Watch out for the word "that", which can be a pronoun or an adjective or a conjunction. And remember that "my", "your", "our" and "their" are always adjectives. [All pronouns in this section are in italics.]

**Prepositions.** Prepositions are the little words that introduce phrases that tell *about* condition, time, place, manner, association, degree and similar topics. Such words as *with, in, beside, under, of, to, about, for* and *upon* are prepositions. In English prepositions and adverbs overlap, but, as you will see *by* checking *in* your dictionary, there are usually differences *of* meaning *between* the two uses. [Prepositions *in* this paragraph are designated *by* italics.]

**Conjunctions.** Conjunctions are joining-words. They enable you to link words *or* groups of words into larger units, *and* to build compound *or* complex sentences out of simple sentence units. Such words as *and, but, although, or, unless* are typical conjunctions. *Although* most conjunctions are easy enough to identify, the word "that" should be watched closely to see *that* it is not a pronoun *or* an adjective. [Conjunctions italicized.]

### Words about Verbs

Verbs are responsible for most of the terminology in this short grammar. The basic terms are:

**Conjugation.** In many languages verbs fall into natural groups, according to the way they make their forms. These groupings are called conjugations, and are an aid to learning grammatical structure. Though it may seem difficult at first to speak of First and Second Conjugations, these are simply short ways of saying that verbs belonging to these classes make their forms according to certain consistent rules, which you can memorize.

**Infinitive.** This is the basic form which most dictionaries give for verbs in most languages, and in most languages it serves as the basis for classifying verbs. In English (with a very few exceptions) it has no special form. To find the infinitive for any English verb, just fill in this sentence: "I like to . . .

(walk, run, jump, swim, carry, disappear, etc.)." The infinitive in English is usually preceded by the word "to".

**Tense.** This is simply a formal way of saying "time". In English we think of time as being broken into three great segments: past, present and future. Our verbs are assigned forms to indicate this division, and are further subdivided for shades of meaning. We subdivide the present time into the present (I walk) and present progressive (I am walking); the past into the simple past (I walked), progressive past (I was walking), perfect or present perfect (I have walked), past perfect or pluperfect (I had walked); and future into simple future (I shall walk) and future progressive (I shall be walking). These are the most common English tenses.

**Present Participles, Progressive Tenses.** In English the present participle always ends in -*ing*. It can be used as a noun or an adjective in some situations, but its chief use is in *forming* the so-called progressive tenses. These are made by *putting* appropriate forms of the verb "to be" before a present participle: For "to walk" [an infinitive], for example, the present progressive would be: I am *walking*, you are *walking*, he is *walking*, etc.; past progressive, I was *walking*, you were *walking* and so on. [Present participles are in italics.]

**Past Participles, Perfect Tenses.** The past participle in English is not *formed* as regularly as is the present participle. Sometimes it is *constructed* by adding -ed or -d to the present tense, as *walked, jumped, looked, received*; but there are many verbs where it is *formed* less regularly: *seen, been, swum, chosen, brought*. To find it, simply fill out the sentence "I have . . ." putting in the verb form that your ear tells you is right for the particular verb. If you speak grammatically you will have the past participle.

Past participles are sometimes used as adjectives: "Don't cry over *spilt* milk." Their most important use, however, is to form the system of verb tenses that are *called* the perfect tenses: present perfect (or perfect), past perfect (or pluperfect), etc. In English the present perfect tense is *formed* with the present tense of "to have" and the past participle of a verb: I have *walked*, you have *run*, he has *begun*, etc. The past perfect is *formed*, similarly, with the past tense of "to have" and the past participle: I had *walked*, you had *run*, he had *begun*. Most of the languages you are likely to study have similar systems of perfect tenses, though they may not be *formed* in exactly the same way as in English. [Past participles in italics.]

**Preterite, Imperfect.** Many languages have more than one verb tense for expressing an action that took place in the past. They may use a perfect tense (which we have just covered), or a preterite, or an imperfect. English, although you may never have thought about it, is one of these languages, for we can say "I have spoken to him" [present perfect], or "I spoke to him" [simple past], or "I was speaking to him" [past progressive]. These sentences do not mean exactly the same thing, although the differences are subtle, and are difficult to put into other words.

While usage differs a little from language to language, if a language has both a preterite and an imperfect, in general the preterite corresponds to the English simple past (I ran, I swam, I spoke), and the imperfect corresponds to the English past progressive (I was running, I was swimming, I was speaking). If you are curious to discover the mode of thought behind these different tenses try looking at the situation in terms of background-action and point-action. One of the most important uses of the imperfect is to provide a background against which a single point-action can take place. For example, "When I was walking down the street [background, continued over a period of time, hence past progressive or imperfect], I stubbed my toe [an instant or point of time, hence a simple past or preterite]."

**Auxiliary Verbs.** Auxiliary verbs are special words that are used to help other verbs make their forms. In English, for example, we use forms of the verb "to have" in our perfect tenses: I have seen, you had come, he has been, etc. We also use shall or will to make our future tenses: I shall pay, you will see, etc. French, German, Spanish and Italian also make use of auxiliary verbs, but although the same general concept is present, the use of auxiliaries differs very much from one language to another, and you must learn the practice for each language.

**Reflexive.** This term, which sounds more difficult than it really is, simply means that the verb refers back to the noun or pronoun that is its subject. In modern English the reflexive pronoun always ends with -*self*, and we do not use the construction very frequently. In other languages, however, reflexive forms may be used more frequently, and in ways that do not seem very logical to an English speaker. Examples of English reflexive sentences: "He washes himself." "He seated himself at the table."

**Passive.** In some languages, like Latin, there is a strong feeling that an action or thing that is taking place can be expressed in two different ways. One can say, A does-something-to B, which is "active"; or B is-having-something-done-to-him by A, which is "passive". We do not have a strong feeling for this classification of experience in English, but the following examples should indicate the difference between an active and a passive verb: Active: "John is building a house." Passive: "A house is being built by John." Active: "The steamer carried the cotton to England." Passive: "The cotton was carried by the steamer to England." Bear in mind that the formation of passive verbs and the situations where they can be used vary enormously from language to language. This is one situation where you usually cannot translate English word for word into another language and make sense.

**Impersonal Verbs.** In English there are some verbs which do not have an ordinary subject, and do not refer to persons. They are always used with the pronoun *it*, which does not refer to anything specifically, but simply serves to fill out the verb forms. Examples: It is snowing. It hailed last night. It seems to me that you are wrong. It has been raining.

Other languages, like German, have this same general concept, but impersonal verbs may differ quite a bit in form and frequency from one language to another.

### Words about Nouns

**Agreement.** In some languages, where nouns or adjectives or articles are declined, or have gender endings, it is necessary that the adjective or article be in the same case or gender or number as the noun it goes with (modifies). This is called agreement.

This may be illustrated from Italian, where articles and adjectives have to agree with nouns in gender and number.

| | | | |
|---|---|---|---|
| una casa rossa | one red house | due case rosse | two red houses |
| un libro rosso | one red book | due libri rossi | two red books |

Here *una* is feminine singular and has the ending -*a* because it agrees with the feminine singular noun *casa*; *rossa* has the ending -*a* because it agrees with the feminine singular noun *casa*. *Rosso*, on the other hand, and *un*, are masculine singular because *libro* is masculine singular.

**Gender.** Gender should not be confused with actual sex. In many languages nouns are arbitrarily assigned a gender (masculine or feminine, or masculine or feminine or neuter), and this need not correspond to sex. You simply have to learn the pattern of the language you are studying in order to become familiar with its use of gender.

## Miscellaneous Terms

**Comparative, Superlative.** These two terms are used with adjectives and adverbs. They indicate the degree of strength within the meaning of the word. Faster, better, earlier, newer, more rapid, more detailed, more suitable are examples of the comparative in adjectives, while more rapidly, more recently, more suitably are comparatives for adverbs.

In most cases, as you have seen, the comparative uses -er or "more" for an adjective, and "more" for an adverb. Superlatives are those forms which end in -est or have "most" placed before them for adjectives, and "most" prefixed for adverbs: most intelligent, earliest, most rapidly, most suitably.

**Idiom.** An idiom is an expression that is peculiar to a language, the meaning of which is not the same as the literal meaning of the individual words composing it. Idioms, as a rule, cannot be translated word by word into another language. Examples of English idioms: *"Take it easy."* "Don't *beat around the bush."* "It *turned out* to be *a Dutch treat."*

## The Parts of the Sentence

**Subject, Predicate.** In grammar *every complete sentence* contains two basic parts, the subject and the predicate. *The subject*, if *we* state the terms most simply, is the thing, person or activity talked about. *It* can be a noun, a pronoun or something *that* serves as a noun. *A subject* would include, in a typical case, a noun, the articles or adjectives *which* are associated with it and perhaps phrases. Note that in complex sentences *each part* may have its own subject. [*The subjects of the sentences above* have been italicized.]

The predicate *talks about the subject.* In a formal sentence the predicate *includes a verb, its adverbs, predicate adjectives, phrases and objects*—whatever *happens to be present.* A predicate adjective *is an adjective* which *happens to be in the predicate after a form of the verb to be.* Example: "Apples *are red."* [Predicates *are in italics.*]

In the following simple sentences subjects are in italics,

predicates in italics and underlined. "*Green apples are bad for your digestion.*" "When *I go to Italy, I always stop in Milan.*" "*The man with the suitcase is travelling to Florence.*"

**Direct and Indirect Objects.** Some verbs (called transitive verbs) take direct and/or indirect objects in their predicates; other verbs (called intransitive verbs) do not take objects of any sort. In English, except for pronouns, objects do not have any special forms, but in languages which have case forms or more pronoun forms than English, objects can be troublesome.

The direct object is the person, thing, quality or matter that the verb directs *its action* upon. It can be a pronoun or a noun, perhaps accompanied by an article and/or adjectives. The direct object always directly follows *its verb*, except when there is also an indirect object pronoun present, which comes between the verb and the object. Prepositions do not go before direct objects. Examples: "The cook threw *green onions* into the stew." "The border guards will want to see *your passport* tomorrow." "Give *it* to me." "Please give me *a glass of red wine*." [We have placed *direct objects* in this paragraph in italics.]

The indirect object, as grammars will tell *you*, is the person or thing for or to whom the action is taking place. It can be a pronoun or a noun with or without article and adjectives. In most cases the words "to" or "for" can be inserted before it, if not already there. Examples: "Please tell *me* the time." "I wrote *her* a letter from Rome." "We sent *Mr. Medoni* ten lire." "We gave *the most energetic guide* a large tip." [Indirect objects are in italics.]

# Index

The following abbreviations have been used in this index: *adj.* for adjective, *def.* for definition, and *pron.* for pronoun. Italian words appear in *italic* and their English equivalents in parentheses.